Android SQLite Essentials

Develop Android applications with one of the most widely used database engines, SQLite

Sunny Kumar Aditya

Vikash Kumar Karn

[PACKT] PUBLISHING

open source community experience distilled

BIRMINGHAM - MUMBAI

Android SQLite Essentials

First published: August 2014

Production reference: 1200814

Published by Packt Publishing Ltd.
Livery Place
35 Livery Street
Birmingham B3 2PB, UK.

ISBN 978-1-78328-295-1

www.packtpub.com

Cover image by Pratyush Mohanta (tysoncinematics@gmail.com)

Credits

Authors
Sunny Kumar Aditya
Vikash Kumar Karn

Reviewers
Amey Haldankar
Gaurav Maru

Commissioning Editor
Pramila Balan

Acquisition Editor
Nikhil Karkal

Content Development Editor
Ruchita Bhansali

Technical Editors
Dennis John
Gaurav Thingalaya

Copy Editors
Roshni Banerjee
Gladson Monteiro
Adithi Shetty

Project Coordinator
Kranti Berde

Proofreaders
Simran Bhogal
Joanna McMahon

Indexers
Mariammal Chettiyar
Rekha Nair

Graphics
Ronak Dhruv

Production Coordinator
Saiprasad Kadam

Cover Work
Saiprasad Kadam

About the Authors

Sunny Kumar Aditya has been working on the Android platform for the past 4 years. His tryst with Android began with his college project, and he continued with his work in R&D at HCL Infosystems Ltd. Sunny loves to stay up to date with the latest trends and practices in Android development. Apart from building Android applications, he writes at `www.deadmango.com`. He is currently the head of Android development at Yamunix.

I would like to thank Packt Publishing for this opportunity and my family as well as friends for their support.

Vikash Kumar Karn is an IIIT Allahabad alumnus and an ECE student whose love for code drove him towards the software development field. He has worked with leading multinationals and is currently working at Samsung Research Institute, Bangalore, exploring Android.

Vikash likes to learn the intricacies of the Android framework and help newcomers in this field. Some of his applications, such as Movtan Fishing and Compare Pictures, can be found on the Play Store.

I would like to thank my friends and family for their support during the course of writing this book.

About the Reviewers

Amey Haldankar is an Android enthusiast hooked on the platform since its early days. Equipped with a degree in Computer Science Engineering from GIT, Belgaum, he is working for HCL Infosystems Ltd. as a Senior Software Engineer.

Amey has been working on the platform for the past 3 years developing several applications for major clients such as Domino's, Galatsaray, HCL, and Nokia.

A note of thanks to the publishing house for considering me for the role of a reviewer for *Android SQLite Essentials*.

Gaurav Maru has a Bachelor's degree in Computers from Shah & Anchor Kutchhi Engineering College. Since 2011, he has been working as an Android application developer at various organizations, including India's largest retail sector company. Gaurav has developed various apps, including the one developed for the USA's largest bookseller (a Fortune 500 company). He drinks, eats, and sleeps Android. You can contact him at `gaurav1maru@gmail.com`.

I would like to thank my family, friends, colleagues, and Packt Publishing, who helped me pull this one off successfully. Cheers!

---

www.PacktPub.com

Support files, eBooks, discount offers and more

You might want to visit www.PacktPub.com for support files and downloads related to your book.

Did you know that Packt offers eBook versions of every book published, with PDF and ePub files available? You can upgrade to the eBook version at www.PacktPub.com and as a print book customer, you are entitled to a discount on the eBook copy. Get in touch with us at service@packtpub.com for more details.

At www.PacktPub.com, you can also read a collection of free technical articles, sign up for a range of free newsletters and receive exclusive discounts and offers on Packt books and eBooks.

PACKTLIB®

http://PacktLib.PacktPub.com

Do you need instant solutions to your IT questions? PacktLib is Packt's online digital book library. Here, you can access, read and search across Packt's entire library of books.

Why Subscribe?

- Fully searchable across every book published by Packt
- Copy and paste, print and bookmark content
- On demand and accessible via web browser

Free Access for Packt account holders

If you have an account with Packt at www.PacktPub.com, you can use this to access PacktLib today and view nine entirely free books. Simply use your login credentials for immediate access.

Table of Contents

Preface

Android is probably the buzzword of this decade. In a short span, it has taken over the majority of the handset market. Android is staged to take over wearables, our TV rooms, as well as our cars this autumn with the Android L release. With the frantic pace at which Android is growing, a developer needs to up his or her skill sets as well. Database-oriented application development is one of the key skills every developer should have. SQLite database in applications is the heart of a data-centric product and key to building great products. Understanding SQLite and implementing the Android database can be a steep learning curve for some people. Concepts such as content providers and loaders are more complex to understand and implement. *Android SQLite Essentials* equips developers with tools to build database-based Android applications in a simplistic manner. It is written keeping in mind the current needs and best practices being followed in the industry. Let us start our journey.

What this book covers

Chapter 1, *Enter SQLite*, provides an insight into SQLite architecture, SQLite basics, and its Android connection.

Chapter 2, *Connecting the Dots*, covers how to connect your database to Android views. It also covers some of the best practices one should follow in order to build a database-centric/database-enabled application.

Chapter 3, *Sharing is Caring*, will reflect on how to access and share data in Android via content providers and how to construct a content provider.

Chapter 4, *Thread Carefully*, will guide you on how to use loaders and ensure security of database and data. It will also provide you with tips to explore alternate approaches to building and using databases in Android applications.

What you need for this book

To efficiently use this book, you will require a working system with Windows, Ubuntu, or Mac OS preinstalled. Download and set up the Java environment; we require this for the IDE of our choice, Eclipse, to run. Download Android SDK from the Android developer's site and Android ADT plugin for Eclipse. Alternatively, you can download the Eclipse ADT bundle that contains Eclipse SDK and the ADT plugin. You can also try Android Studio; this IDE, which just moved to beta, is also available on the developer site. Make sure your operating system, JDK, and IDE are all of either 32 bit or 64 bit.

Who this book is for

Android SQLite Essentials is a guide book for Android programmers who want to explore SQLite database-based Android applications. The reader is expected to have a little bit of hands-on experience of Android fundamental building blocks and the know-how of IDE and Android tools.

Conventions

In this book, you will find a number of styles of text that distinguish between different kinds of information. Here are some examples of these styles and an explanation of their meaning.

Code words in text, database table names, folder names, filenames, file extensions, pathnames, dummy URLs, user input, and Twitter handles are shown as follows: "To close the `Cursor` object, the `close()` method call will be used."

A block of code is set as follows:

```
ContentValues cv = new ContentValues();
cv.put(COL_NAME, "john doe");
cv.put(COL_NUMBER, "12345000");
dataBase.insert(TABLE_CONTACTS, null, cv);
```

Any command-line input or output is written as follows:

```
adb shell SQLite3 --version
SQLite 3.7.11: API 16 - 19
SQLite 3.7.4: API 11 - 15
SQLite 3.6.22: API 8 - 10
SQLite 3.5.9: API 3 - 7
```

New terms and **important words** are shown in bold. Words that you see on the screen, in menus or dialog boxes for example, appear in the text like this: "Go to **Android Virtual Device Manager** from the **Windows** menu to start the emulator."

> Warnings or important notes appear in a box like this.

> Tips and tricks appear like this.

Reader feedback

Feedback from our readers is always welcome. Let us know what you think about this book—what you liked or may have disliked. Reader feedback is important for us to develop titles that you really get the most out of.

To send us general feedback, simply send an e-mail to `feedback@packtpub.com`, and mention the book title via the subject of your message.

If there is a topic that you have expertise in and you are interested in either writing or contributing to a book, see our author guide on `www.packtpub.com/authors`.

Customer support

Now that you are the proud owner of a Packt book, we have a number of things to help you to get the most from your purchase.

Downloading the example code

You can download the example code files for all Packt books you have purchased from your account at `http://www.packtpub.com`. If you purchased this book elsewhere, you can visit `http://www.packtpub.com/support` and register to have the files e-mailed directly to you.

Errata

Although we have taken every care to ensure the accuracy of our content, mistakes do happen. If you find a mistake in one of our books—maybe a mistake in the text or the code—we would be grateful if you would report this to us. By doing so, you can save other readers from frustration and help us improve subsequent versions of this book. If you find any errata, please report them by visiting `http://www.packtpub.com/submit-errata`, selecting your book, clicking on the **errata submission form** link, and entering the details of your errata. Once your errata are verified, your submission will be accepted and the errata will be uploaded on our website, or added to any list of existing errata, under the Errata section of that title. Any existing errata can be viewed by selecting your title from `http://www.packtpub.com/support`.

Piracy

Piracy of copyright material on the Internet is an ongoing problem across all media. At Packt, we take the protection of our copyright and licenses very seriously. If you come across any illegal copies of our works, in any form, on the Internet, please provide us with the location address or website name immediately so that we can pursue a remedy.

Please contact us at `copyright@packtpub.com` with a link to the suspected pirated material.

We appreciate your help in protecting our authors, and our ability to bring you valuable content.

Questions

You can contact us at `questions@packtpub.com` if you are having a problem with any aspect of the book, and we will do our best to address it.

1
Enter SQLite

Dr. Richard Hipp, the architect and primary author of SQLite, explains how it all began in his interview with *The Guardian* published in June 2007:

> *"I started on May 29 2000. It's just over seven years old," he says. He was working on a project which used a database server, but from time to time the database went offline. "Then my program would give an error message saying that the database isn't working, and I got the blame for this. So I said, this is not a demanding application for the database, why don't I just talk directly to the disk, and build an SQL database engine that way? That was how it started."*

Before we begin our journey exploring SQLite in the context of Android, we would like to inform you of some prerequisites. The following are very basic requirements and will require little effort from you:

- You need to ensure that the environment for building Android applications is in place. When we say "environment," we refer to the combination of JDK and Eclipse, our IDE choice, ADT plugins, and Android SDK tools. In case these are not in place, the ADT bundle, which consists of IDE, ADT plugins, Android SDK tools, and platform tools, can be downloaded from `http://developer.android.com/sdk/index.html`. The steps mentioned in the link are pretty self-explanatory. For JDK, you can visit Oracle's website to download the latest version and set it up at `http://www.oracle.com/technetwork/java/javase/downloads/index.html`.

- You need to have a basic knowledge of Android components and have run more than "Hello World" programs on an Android emulator. If not, a very apt guide is present on the Android developer site to set up an emulator. We would suggest you become familiar with basic Android components: Intent, Service, Content Providers, and Broadcast Receiver. The Android developer site has good repositories of samples along with documentation. Some of these are as follows:
    - **Emulator**: `http://developer.android.com/tools/devices/index.html`
    - **Android basics**: `http://developer.android.com/training/basics/firstapp/index.html`

With these things in place, we can now start our foray into SQLite.

In this chapter, we will cover the following:

- Why SQLite?
- The SQLite architecture
- A quick review of database fundamentals
- SQLite in Android

Why SQLite?

SQLite is an embedded SQL database engine. It is used by prominent names such as Adobe in Adobe Integrated Runtime (AIR); Airbus, in their flight software; Python ships with SQLite; PHP; and many more. In the mobile domain, SQLite is a very popular choice across various platforms because of its lightweight nature. Apple uses it in the iPhone and Google in the Android operating system.

It is used as an application file format, a database for electronic gadgets, a database for websites, and as an enterprise RDBMS. What makes SQLite such an interesting choice for these and many other companies? Let's take a closer look at the features of SQLite that make it so popular:

- **Zero-configuration**: SQLite is designed in such a manner that it requires no configuration file. It requires no installation steps or initial setup; it has no server process running and no recovery steps to take even if it crashes. There is no server and it is directly embedded in our application. Furthermore, no administrator is required to create or maintain a DB instance, or set permissions for users. In short, this is a true DBA-less database.

- **No-copyright**: SQLite, instead of a license, comes with a blessing. The source code of SQLite is in the public domain; you are free to modify, distribute, and even sell the code. Even the contributors are asked to sign an affidavit to protect from any copyrights warfare that may occur in future.
- **Cross-platform**: Database files from one system can be moved to a system running a different architecture without any hassle. This is possible because the database file format is binary and all the machines use the same format. In the following chapters, we will be pulling out a database from an Android emulator to Windows.
- **Compact**: An SQLite database is a single ordinary disk file; it comes without a server and is designed to be lightweight and simple. These attributes lead to a very lightweight database engine. SQLite Version 3.7.8 has a footprint of less than 350 KiB (kibibyte) compared to its other SQL database engines, which are much larger.
- **Fool proof**: The code base is well commented, easy to understand, and modular. The test cases and test scripts in SQLite have approximately 1084 times more code than the source code of SQLite library and they claim 100 percent branch test coverage. This level of testing reaffirms the faith instilled in SQLite by developers.

> Interested readers can read more about branch test coverage from Wikipedia at `http://en.wikipedia.org/wiki/Code_coverage`.

The SQLite architecture

The core, SQL compiler, backend, and database form the SQLite architecture:

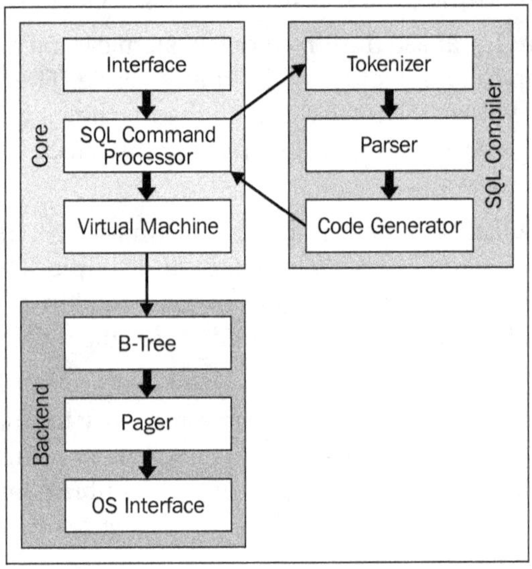

The SQLite interface

At the top of the SQLite library stack, according to documentation, much of the public interface to the SQLite library is implemented by the `wen.c`, `legacy.c`, and `vdbeapi.c` source files. This is the point of communication for other programs and scripts.

The SQL compiler

Tokenizer breaks the SQL string passed from the interface into tokens and hands the tokens over to the parser, one by one. Tokenizer is hand-coded in C. The parser for SQLite is generated by the Lemon parser generator. It is faster than YACC and Bison and, at the same time, is thread safe and prevents memory leaks. The parser builds a parse tree from the tokens passed by the tokenizer and passes the tree to the code generator. The generator produces virtual machine code from the input and passes it to the virtual machine as executables. More information about the Lemon parser generator can be found at `http://en.wikipedia.org/wiki/Lemon_Parser_Generator`.

The virtual machine

The virtual machine, also known as **Virtual Database Engine** (**VDBE**), is the heart of SQLite. It is responsible for fetching and changing values in the database. It executes the program generated by the code generator to manipulate database files. Each SQL statement is first converted into virtual machine language for VDBE. Each instruction of VDBE contains an opcode and up to three additional operands.

The SQLite backend

B-trees, along with Pager and the OS Interface, form the backend of the SQLite architecture. B-trees are used to organize the data. The pager on the other hand assists B-tree by caching, modifying, and rolling back data. B-tree, when required, requests particular pages from the cache; this request is processed by the pager in an efficient and reliable manner. The OS Interface, as the name suggests, provides an abstraction layer to port to different operating systems. It hides the unnecessary details of communicating with different operating systems from SQLite calls and handles them on behalf of SQLite.

These are the internals of SQLite and an application developer in Android need not worry about the internals of Android because the SQLite Android libraries have effectively used the concept of abstraction and all the complexities are hidden. One just needs to master the APIs provided, and that will cater to all the possible use cases of SQLite in an Android application.

A quick review of database fundamentals

A database, in simple words, is an organized way to store data in a continual fashion. Data is saved in tables. A table consists of columns with different datatypes. Every row in a table corresponds to a data record. You may think of a table as an Excel spreadsheet. From the perspective of object-oriented programming, every table in a database usually describes an object (represented by a class). Each table column illustrates a class attribute. Every record in a table represents a particular instance of that object.

Let's look at a quick example. Let's assume you have a Shop database with a table called Inventory. This table might be used to store the information about all the products in the shops. The Inventory table might contain these columns: Product name (string), Product Id (number), Cost (number), In stock (0/1), and Numbers available (number). You could then add a record to the database for a product named Shoe:

ID	Product name	Product Id	Cost	In stock	Numbers available
1	Carpet	340023	2310	1	4
2	Shoe	231257	235	1	2

Data in the database is supposed to be checked and influenced. The data within a table can be as follows:

- Added (with the INSERT command)
- Modified (with the UPDATE command)
- Removed (with the DELETE command)

You may search for particular data within a database by utilizing what is known as a **query**. A query (using the SELECT command) can involve one table, or a number of tables. To generate a query, you must determine the tables, data columns, and values of the data of interest using SQL commands. Each SQL command is concluded with a semicolon (;).

What is an SQLite statement?

An SQLite statement is written in SQL, which is issued to a database to retrieve data or to create, insert, update, or delete data in the database.

All SQLite statements start with any of the keywords: SELECT, INSERT, UPDATE, DELETE, ALTER, DROP, and so on, and all the statements end with a semicolon (;). For instance:

```
CREATE TABLE table_name (column_name INTEGER);
```

The CREATE TABLE command is used to create a new table in an SQLite database. A CREATE TABLE command describes the following attributes of the new table that is being created:

- The name of the new table.
- The database in which the new table is created. Tables may be generated in the main database, the temp database, or in any database attached.
- The name of each column in the table.

- The declared type of each colum
- A default value or expression fo
- A default relation sequence to b
- Preferably, a PRIMARY KEY for t and composite (multiple-colum
- A set of SQL constraints for eac NULL, CHECK, and FOREIGN KEY
- In some cases, the table will be

The following is a simple SQLite state

```
String databaseTable =   "CREA
   + TABLE_CONTACTS +"("
   + KEY_ID
   + " INTEGER PRIMARY KEY,"
   + KEY_NAME + " TEXT,"
   + KEY_NUMBER + " INTEGER"
   + ")";
```

Here, CREATE TABLE is the command to create a table with the name TABLE_CONTACTS. KEY_ID, KEY_NAME and KEY_NUMBER are the column IDs. SQLite requires a unique ID to be provided for each column. INTEGER and TEXT are the datatypes associated with the corresponding columns. SQLite requires the type of data to be stored in a column to be defined at the time of creation of the table. PRIMARY KEY is the data column **constraint** (rules enforced on data columns in the table).

SQLite supports more attributes that can be used for creating a table, for instance, let us create a create table statement that inputs a default value for empty columns. Notice that for KEY_NAME, we are providing a default value as xyz and for the KEY_NUMBER column, we are providing a default value of 100:

```
String databaseTable =
   "CREATE TABLE "
   + TABLE_CONTACTS  + "("
   + KEY_ID    + " INTEGER PRIMARY KEY,"


   + KEY_NAME + " TEXT DEFAULT  xyz,"

   + KEY_NUMBER + " INTEGER DEFAULT 100" + ")";
```

Here, when a row is inserted in the database, these columns will be preinitialized with the default values as defined in the CREATE SQL statement.

e don't want you to get bored with a huge list. We ds in the subsequent chapters.

yntax

ique set of rules and guidelines called **syntax**.

oint to be noted is that SQLite is **case-insensitive**, but there are nds that are case-sensitive, for example, `GLOB` and `glob` have different n SQLite. Let us look at the SQLite `DELETE` statement's syntax for instance. gh we have used capital letters, replacing them with lowercase letters will work fine:

```
DELETE FROM table WHERE {condition};
```

Datatypes in SQLite

SQLite uses a dynamic and weakly typed SQL syntax, whereas most of the SQL databases use static, rigid typing. If we look at other languages, Java is a statically typed language and Python is a dynamically typed language. So what do we mean when we say dynamic or static? Let us look at an example:

```
a=5
a="android"
```

In statically typed languages, this will throw an exception, whereas in a dynamically typed language it will work. In SQLite, the datatype of a value is not associated with its container, but with the value itself. This is not a cause of concern when dealing with statically typed systems, where a value is determined by a container. This is because SQLite is backwards compatible with the more common static type systems. Hence, the SQL statements that we use for static systems can be used seamlessly here.

Storage classes

In SQLite, we have **storage** classes that are more general than datatypes. Internally, SQLite stores data in five storage classes that can also be referred to as **primitive datatypes**:

- `NULL`: This represents a missing value from the database.
- `INTEGER`: This supports a range of signed integers from 1, 2, 3, 4, 6, or 8 bytes depending on the magnitude of the value. SQLite handles this automatically based on the value. At the time of processing in the memory, they are converted to the most general 8-byte signed integer form.

- `REAL`: This is a floating point value, and SQLite uses this as an 8-byte IEEE floating point number to store such values.
- `TEXT`: SQLite supports various character encodings, such as UTF-8, UTF-16BE, or UTF-16LE. This value is a text string.
- `BLOB`: This type stores a large array of binary data, exactly how it was provided as input.

SQLite itself does not validate if the types written to the columns are actually of the defined type, for example, you can write an integer into a string column and vice versa. We can even have a single column with different storage classes:

```
 id                  col_t
------              ------
1                     23
2                   NULL
3                   test
```

The Boolean datatype

SQLite does not have a separate storage class for Boolean and uses the `Integer` class for this purpose. Integer `0` represents the false state whereas `1` represents a true state. This means that there is an indirect support for Boolean and we can create Boolean type columns only. The catch is, it won't contain the familiar `TRUE/FALSE` values.

The Date and Time datatype

As we saw for the Boolean datatype, there is no storage class for the Date and Time datatypes in SQLite. SQLite has five built-in date and time functions to help us with it; we can use date and time as integer, text, or real values. Moreover, the values are interchangeable, depending on the need of the application. For example, to compute the current date, use the following code:

```
SELECT date('now');
```

SQLite in Android

The Android software stack consists of core Linux kernel, Android runtime, Android libraries that support the Android framework, and finally Android applications that run on top of everything. The Android runtime uses **Dalvik virtual machine** (**DVM**) to execute the dex code. In newer versions of Android, that is, from KitKat (4.4), Android has enabled an experimental feature known as **ART**, which will eventually replace DVM. It is based on **Ahead of Time** (**AOT**), whereas DVM is based on **Just in Time** (**JIT**). In the following diagram, we can see that SQLite provides native database support and is part of the libraries that support the application framework along with libraries such as SSL, OpenGL ES, WebKit, and so on. These libraries, written in C/C++, run over the Linux kernel and, along with the Android runtime, forms the backbone of the application framework, as shown in the following diagram:

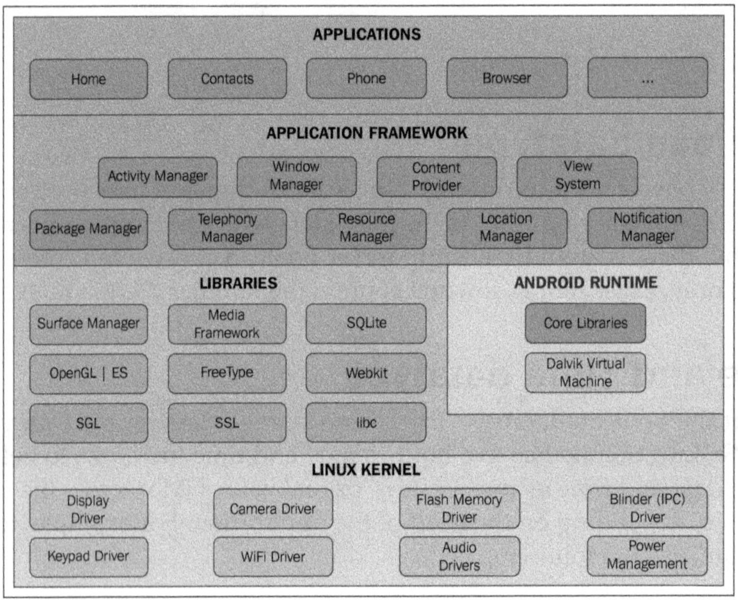

Before we start exploring SQLite in Android, let's take a look at the other persistent storage alternatives in Android:

- **Shared preference**: Data is stored in a shared preference in the key-value form. The file itself is an XML file containing the key-value pairs. The file is present in the internal storage of an application, and access to it can be public or private as needed. Android provides APIs to write and read shared preferences. It is advised to use this in case we have to save a small collection of such data. A general example would be saving the last read position in a PDF, or saving a user's preference to show a rating box.

- **Internal/external storage**: This terminology can be a little misleading; Android defines two storage spaces to save files. On some devices, you might have an external storage device in form of an SD card, whereas on others, you will find that the system has partitioned its memory into two parts, to be labeled as internal and external. Paths to the external as well as internal storage can be fetched by using Android APIs. Internal storage, by default, is limited and accessible only to the application, whereas the external storage may or may not be available in case it is mounted.

> `android:installLocation` can be used in the manifest to specify the internal/external installation location of an application.

SQLite version

Since API level 1, Android ships with SQLite. At the time of writing this book, the current version of SQLite was 3.8.4.1. According to the documentation, the version of SQLite is 3.4.0, but different Android versions are known to ship with different versions of SQLite. We can easily verify this via the use of a tool called **SQLite3** present in the `platform-tools` folder inside the Android SDK installation folder and Android Emulator:

```
adb shell SQLite3 --version
SQLite 3.7.11: API 16 - 19
SQLite 3.7.4: API 11 - 15
SQLite 3.6.22: API 8 - 10
SQLite 3.5.9: API 3 - 7
```

We need not worry about the different versions of SQLite and should stick to 3.5.9 for compatibility, or we can go by the saying that API 14 is the new `minSdkVersion` and switch it with 3.7.4. Until and unless you have something very specific to a particular version, it will hardly matter.

> Some additional handy SQLite3 commands are as follows:
>
> - `.dump`: To print out the contents of a table
> - `.schema`: To print the `SQL CREATE` statement for an existing table
> - `.help`: For instructions

Database packages

The `android.database` package contains all the necessary classes for working with databases. The `android.database.SQLite` package contains the SQLite-specific classes.

APIs

Android provides various APIs to enable us to create, access, modify, and delete a database. The complete list can be quite overwhelming; for the sake of brevity, we will cover the most important and used ones.

The SQLiteOpenHelper class

The `SQLiteOpenHelper` class is the first and most essential class of Android to work with SQLite databases; it is present in the `android.database.SQLite` namespace. `SQLiteOpenHelper` is a helper class that is designed for extension and to implement the tasks and actions you deem important when creating, opening, and using a database. This helper class is provided by the Android framework to work with the SQLite database and helps in managing the database creation and version management. The modus operandi would be to extend the class and implement tasks and actions as required by our application. `SQLiteOpenHelper` has constructors defined as follows:

```
SQLiteOpenHelper(Context context, String name, SQLiteDatabase.
CursorFactory factory, int version)

SQLiteOpenHelper(Context context, String name, SQLiteDatabase.
CursorFactory factory, int version, DatabaseErrorHandler errorHandler)
```

The application context permits access to all the shared resources and assets for the application. The `name` parameter consists of the database filename in the Android storage. `SQLiteDatabase.CursorFactory` is a factory class that creates cursor objects that act as the output set for all the queries you apply against SQLite under Android. The application-specific version number for the database will be the version parameter (or more particularly, its schema).

The constructor of `SQLiteOpenHelper` is used to create a helper object to create, open, or manage a database. The **context** is the application context that allows access to all the shared resources and assets. The `name` parameter either contains the name of a database or null for an in-memory database. The `SQLiteDatabase.CursorFactory` factory creates a cursor object that acts as the result set for all the queries. The `version` parameter defines the version number of the database and is used to upgrade/downgrade the database. The `errorHandler` parameter in the second constructor is used when SQLite reports database corruption.

`SQLiteOpenHelper` will trigger its `onUpgrade()` method if our database version number is not at default `1`. Important methods of the `SQLiteOpenHelper` class are as follows:

- `synchronized void close()`
- `synchronized SQLiteDatabase getReadableDatabase()`
- `synchronized SQLiteDatabase getWritableDatabase()`
- `abstract void onCreate(SQLiteDatabase db)`
- `void onOpen(SQLiteDatabase db)`
- `abstract void onUpgrade(SQLiteDatabase db, int oldVersion, int newVersion)`

The synchronized `close()` method closes any open database object. The `synchronized` keyword prevents thread and memory consistency errors.

The next two methods, `getReadableDatabase()` and `getWriteableDatabase()`, are the methods in which the database is actually created or opened. Both return the same `SQLiteDatabase` object; the difference lies in the fact that `getReadableDatabase()` will return a readable database in case it cannot return a writable database, whereas `getWriteableDatabase()` returns a writable database object. The `getWriteableDatabase()` method will throw an `SQLiteException` if a database cannot be opened for writing. In case of `getReadableDatabase()`, if a database cannot be opened, it will throw the same exception.

We can use the `isReadOnly()` method of the `SQLiteDatabase` class on the database object to know the state of the database. It returns `true` for read-only databases.

Calling either methods will invoke the `onCreate()` method if the database doesn't exist yet. Otherwise, it will invoke the `onOpen()` or `onUpgrade()` methods, depending on the version number. The `onOpen()` method should check the `isReadOnly()` method before updating the database. Once opened, the database is cached to improve performance. Finally, we need to call the `close()` method to close the database object.

The `onCreate()`, `onOpen()`, and `onUpgrade()` methods are designed for the subclass to implement the intended behavior. The `onCreate()` method is called when the database is created for the first time. This is the place where we create our tables by using SQLite statements, which we saw earlier in the example. The `onOpen()` method is triggered when the database has been configured and after the database schema has been created, upgraded, or downgraded as necessary. Read/write status should be checked here with the help of the `isReadOnly()` method.

The `onUpgrade()` method is called when the database needs to be upgraded depending on the version number supplied to it. By default, the database version is `1`, and as we increment the database version numbers and release new versions, the upgrade will be performed.

A simple example illustrating the use of the SQLiteOpenHelper class is present in the code bundle for this chapter; we would be using it for explanation:

```
class SQLiteHelperClass
    {
        ...
        ...
        public static final int VERSION_NUMBER = 1;

        sqlHelper =
           new SQLiteOpenHelper(context, "ContactDatabase", null,
          VERSION_NUMBER)
        {

          @Override
          public void onUpgrade(SQLiteDatabase db,
                int oldVersion, int newVersion)
          {

            //drop table on upgrade
            db.execSQL("DROP TABLE IF EXISTS "
                    + TABLE_CONTACTS);
            // Create tables again
            onCreate(db);

          }

       @Override
       public void onCreate(SQLiteDatabase db)
       {
          // creating table during onCreate
          String createContactsTable =
     "CREATE TABLE "
     + TABLE_CONTACTS + "("
     + KEY_ID + " INTEGER PRIMARY KEY,"
     + KEY_NAME + " TEXT,"
     + KEY_NUMBER + " INTEGER" + ")";

            try {
           db.execSQL(createContactsTable);
            } catch(SQLException e) {
              e.printStackTrace();
```

```
            }
        }

        @Override
        public synchronized void close()
        {
            super.close();
            Log.d("TAG", "Database closed");
        }

        @Override
        public void onOpen(SQLiteDatabase db)
        {
                super.onOpen(db);
                Log.d("TAG", "Database opened");
        }

    };

    ...
    ...

    //open the database in read-only mode
    SQLiteDatabase db = SQLiteOpenHelper.getWritableDatabase();

    ...
    ...

    //open the database in read/write mode
    SQLiteDatabase db = SQLiteOpenHelper.getWritableDatabase();
```

Downloading the example code

You can download the example code files for all Packt books you have purchased from your account at `http://www.packtpub.com`. If you purchased this book elsewhere, you can visit `http://www.packtpub.com/support` and register to have the files e-mailed directly to you.

The SQLiteDatabase class

Now that you are familiar with the helper class that kick-starts the use of SQLite databases within Android, it's time to look at the core `SQLiteDatabase` class. `SQLiteDatabase` is the base class required to work with an SQLite database in Android and provides methods to open, query, update, and close the database.

More than 50 methods are available for the `SQLiteDatabase` class, each with its own nuances and use cases. Rather than an exhaustive list, we'll cover the most important subsets of methods and allow you to explore some of the overloaded methods at your leisure. At any time, you can refer to the full online Android documentation for the `SQLiteDatabase` class at `http://developer.android.com/reference/android/database/SQLite/SQLiteDatabase.html`.

Some methods of the `SQLiteDatabase` class are shown in the following list:

- `public long insert (String table, String nullColumnHack, ContentValues values)`
- `public Cursor query (String table, String[] columns, String selection, String[] selectionArgs, String groupBy, String having, String orderBy)`
- `public Cursor rawQuery(String sql, String[] selectionArgs)`
- `public int delete (String table, String whereClause, String[] whereArgs)`
- `public int update (String table, ContentValues values, String whereClause, String[] whereArgs)`

Let us see these `SQLiteDatabase` classes in action with an example. We will insert a name and number in our table. Then we will use the raw query to fetch data back from the table. After this, we will go through the `delete()` and `update()` methods, both of which will take `id` as a parameter to identify which row of data in our database table we intend to delete or update:

```
public void insertToSimpleDataBase()
{
   SQLiteDatabase db = sqlHelper.getWritableDatabase();

   ContentValues cv = new ContentValues();
   cv.put(KEY_NAME, "John");
   cv.put(KEY_NUMBER, "0000000000");
   // Inserting values in different columns of the table using
   // Content Values
   db.insert(TABLE_CONTACTS, null, cv);

   cv = new ContentValues();
   cv.put(KEY_NAME, "Tom");
   cv.put(KEY_NUMBER, "5555555");
   // Inserting values in different columns of the table using
   // Content Values
   db.insert(TABLE_CONTACTS, null, cv);
}
...
```

```
...

public void getDataFromDatabase()
{
   int count;
   db = sqlHelper.getReadableDatabase();
   // Use of normal query to fetch data
   Cursor cr = db. query(TABLE_CONTACTS, null, null,
                        null, null, null, null);

   if(cr != null) {
      count = cr.getCount();
      Log.d("DATABASE", "count is : " + count);
   }

   // Use of raw query to fetch data
   cr = db.rawQuery("select * from " + TABLE_CONTACTS, null);
   if(cr != null) {
      count = cr.getCount();
      Log.d("DATABASE", "count is : " + count);
   }

}
...
...

public void delete(String name)
 {
     String whereClause = KEY_NAME + "=?";
     String[] whereArgs = new String[]{name};
     db = sqlHelper.getWritableDatabase();
     int rowsDeleted = db.delete(TABLE_CONTACTS, whereClause,
whereArgs);
 }
...
...

public void update(String name)
 {
     String whereClause = KEY_NAME + "=?";
     String[] whereArgs = new String[]{name};
     ContentValues cv = new ContentValues();
     cv.put(KEY_NAME, "Betty");
     cv.put(KEY_NUMBER, "999000");
     db = sqlHelper.getWritableDatabase();
     int rowsUpdated = db.update(TABLE_CONTACTS, cv, whereClause,
whereArgs);
 }
```

ContentValues

`ContentValues` is essentially a set of key-value pairs, where the key represents the column for the table and the value is the value to be inserted in that column. So, in the case of `values.put("COL_1", 1);`, the column is `COL_1` and the value being inserted for that column is `1`.

The following is an example:

```
ContentValues cv = new ContentValues();
cv.put(COL_NAME, "john doe");
cv.put(COL_NUMBER, "12345000");
dataBase.insert(TABLE_CONTACTS, null, cv);
```

Cursor

A query recovers a `Cursor` object. A `Cursor` object depicts the result of a query and fundamentally points to one row of the result of the query. With this method, Android can buffer the results of the query in a productive manner; as it doesn't need to load all of the data into memory.

To obtain the elements of the resulting query, you can use the `getCount()` method.

To navigate amid individual data rows, you can utilize the `moveToFirst()` and `moveToNext()` methods. The `isAfterLast()` method permits you to analyze whether the end of the output has arrived.

The `Cursor` object provides typed `get*()` methods, for example, the `getLong(columnIndex)` and `getString(columnIndex)` methods to gain entry to the column data for the ongoing position of the result. `columnIndex` is the number of the column you will be accessing.

The `Cursor` object also provides the `getColumnIndexOrThrow(String)` method that permits you to get the column index for a column name of the table.

To close the `Cursor` object, the `close()` method call will be used.

A database query returns a cursor. This interface provides random read-write access to the result set. It points to a row of the query result that enables Android to buffer the results effectively since now it is not required to load all the data in the memory.

The pointer of the returned cursor points to the 0th location, which is known as the first location of the cursor. We need to call the `moveToFirst()` method on the `Cursor` object; it takes the cursor pointer to the first location. Now we can access the data present in the first record.

Cursor implementations, if from multiple threads, should perform their own synchronization when using the cursor. A cursor needs to be closed to free the resource the object holds by calling the `close()` method.

Some other support methods we will encounter are as follows:

- The `getCount()` method: This returns the numbers of elements in the resulting query.
- The `get*()` methods: These are used to access the column data for the current position of the result, for example, `getLong(columnIndex)` and `getString(columnIndex)`.
- The `moveToNext()` method: This moves the cursor to the next row. If the cursor is already past the last entry in the result set, it will return `false`.

Summary

We covered in this chapter the know-how of SQLite features and its internal architecture. We started with a discussion on what makes SQLite so popular by looking at its salient features, then we covered the underlying architecture of SQLite and went over database fundamentals such as syntax and datatypes, and finally moved on to SQLite in Android. We explored the Android APIs for using SQLite in Android.

In the next chapter, we will focus on carrying forward what we have learned in this chapter and apply it to build Android applications. We will focus on the UI elements and connecting UI to the database components.

2
Connecting the Dots

"You don't understand anything until you learn it more than one way."

-Marvin Minsky

In the previous chapter, we learned the two important Android classes and their corresponding methods in order to work with an SQLite database:

- The `SQLiteOpenHelper` class
- The `SQLiteDatabase` class

We also saw code snippets explaining their implementation. Now, we are ready to use all these concepts in an Android application. We will be leveraging what we learned in the previous chapter to make a functional application. We will further look into the SQL statements to insert, query, and delete data from a database.

In this chapter, we will be building and running an Android application on an Android emulator. We will also be building our own full-fledged `contacts` database. We will encounter Android UI components, such as `Buttons` and `ListView`, while progressing through this chapter. In case a revisit of UI components in Android is required, please visit the link `http://developer.android.com/design/building-blocks/index.html`.

Before we begin, the code in this chapter is meant to explain the concepts related to an SQLite database in Android and is not production ready; in a lot of places, you will find lack of proper exception handling or lack of proper null checks and similar practices to reduce verbosity in the code. You can download the complete code from Packt's website for the current and following chapters. For best results, we recommend downloading the code and referring to it as we move along the chapter.

In this chapter, we will cover:

- Building blocks
- Database handler and queries
- Connecting the UI and database

Building blocks

Android is known to run on a variety of devices with different hardware and software specifications. At the time of writing this book, 1 billion activation marks have been crossed. The number of devices running Android is staggering, providing users with a rich variety of options in different form factors and on different hardware bases. This adds a roadblock when it comes to testing your application on different devices, because it is humanly impossible to get hold of them all, not to forget the time and capital needed to be invested in it. Emulator in itself is a great tool; it enables us to circumvent this problem by giving us the flexibility to mimic different hardware features, such as CPU architecture, RAM, and camera, and different software versions ranging from early Cupcake to KitKat. We will also try to leverage this to our advantage in our project and try to run our application on the emulator. An added benefit of using the emulator is that we will be running a rooted device that will allow us to perform some actions. We will not be able to achieve these actions on a normal device.

Let's start by setting up an emulator in Eclipse:

1. Go to **Android Virtual Device Manager** from the **Window** menu to start the emulator.

   We can set different hardware properties such as the CPU type, front/back camera, RAM preferably less than 768 MB on a Windows machine, internal, and external storage size.

2. While launching the app, enable **Save to snapshot**; this will reduce the launch time the next time we are launching an emulator instance from the snapshot:

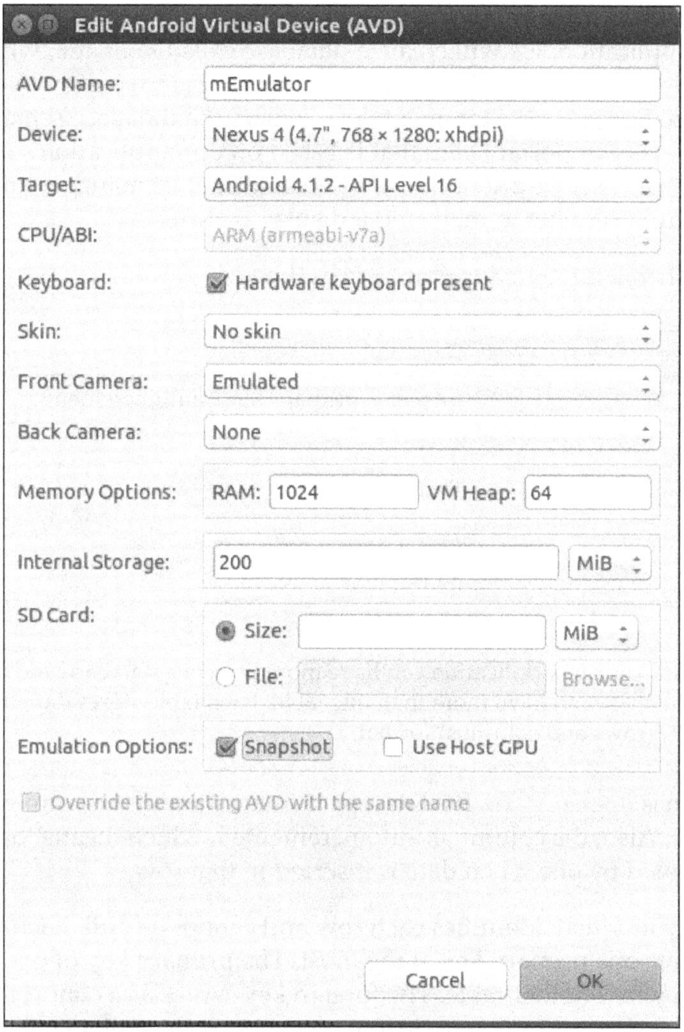

[Interested readers who want to try out a faster emulator can give Genymotion a try at `http://www.genymotion.com/`.]

Let's start building our Android application now.

3. We will start by creating a new project `PersonalContactManager`. Go to **File** | **New** | **Project**. Now, navigate to **Android** and then select **Android Application Project**. This step will give us an activity file and a corresponding XML file.

We will come back to these components after we have all the blocks we need in place. For our application, we will create a database called `contact`, which will contain one table, `ContactsTable`. In the previous chapter, we went over how to create a database using a SQL statement; let's construct a database schema for our project. This is a very important step that is based on our application's requirements; for example, in our case, we are building a personal contact manager and will require fields such as name, number, e-mail, and a display picture.

The database schema for `ContactsTable` is outlined:

Column	**Data type**
`Contact_ID`	Integer / primary key/ autoincrement
`Name`	Text
`Number`	Text
`Email`	Text
`Photo`	Blob

> An Android application can have more than one database and each database can have more than one table. Each table stores data in the 2D (rows and columns) format.

The first column is `Contact_ID`. Its datatype is integer and its **column constraint** is the primary key. Also, the column is autoincremented, which means for each row it will be incremented by one when data is inserted in that row.

The primary key uniquely identifies each row and cannot be null. Each table in a database can have one primary key at the most. The primary key of one table can act as the foreign key for another table. The foreign key serves as a connection between two related tables; for instance, our current `ContactsTable` schema is:

```
ContactsTable (Contact_ID,Name, Number, Email, Photo)
```

Let's say we have another table `ColleagueTable` with the following schema:

```
ColleagueTable (Colleague_ID, Contact_ID, Position, Fax)
```

Here, the primary key of `ContactTable`, that is, `Contact_ID` can be termed as a foreign key for `ColleagueTable`. It serves the purpose of linking two tables in a relational database and hence allows us to perform operations on `ColleagueTable`. We will explore this concept in detail in the chapters and examples ahead.

> **Column constraint**
>
> Constraints are the rules enforced on data columns in a table. This ensures the accuracy and reliability of data in the database.
>
> Unlike most SQL databases, SQLite does not restrict the type of data that may be inserted into a column based on the declared type of columns. Instead, SQLite uses **dynamic typing**. The declared type of a column is used to determine the **affinity** of the column only. There is a type conversion also (automatically) when one type of variable is stored in the other.
>
> Constraints can be column level or table level. Column-level constraints are applied only to one column, whereas table-level constraints are applied to the whole table.
>
> The following are the commonly used constraints and keywords available in SQLite:
>
> - The `NOT NULL` constraint: This ensures that a column does not have a `NULL` value.
> - The `DEFAULT` constraint : This provides a default value for a column when none is specified.
> - The `UNIQUE` constraint: This ensures that all the values in a column are different.
> - The `PRIMARY` key: This uniquely identifies all rows/records in a database table.
> - The `CHECK` constraint: The `CHECK` constraint ensures that all the values in a column satisfy certain conditions.
> - The `AUTO INCREMENT` keyword: `AUTOINCREMENT` is a keyword used to autoincrement a value of a field in the table. We can autoincrement a field value by using the `AUTOINCREMENT` keyword when creating a table with a specific column name to autoincrement it. The keyword `AUTOINCREMENT` can be used with the `INTEGER` field only.

The next step is to prepare our data model; we will use our schema to frame the data model class. The `ContactModel` class will have `Contact_ID`, `Name`, `Number`, `Email`, and `Photo` as fields, they are represented as `id`, `name`, `contactNo`, `email`, and `byteArray` respectively. The class will consist of a getter/setter method to set and fetch property values as needed. The use of a data model will facilitate in the communication of the activity used to show/process data and our database handler, which we are going to define later in this chapter. We will create a new package and a new class in it called the `ContactModel` class. Please note that creating a new package is not a necessary step; it is used to organize our classes in a logical and easily accessible manner. This class can be described as follows:

```
public class ContactModel {
  private int id;
```

```
    private String name, contactNo, email;
    private byte[] byteArray;

    public byte[] getPhoto() {
      return byteArray;
    }
    public void setPhoto(byte[] array) {
      byteArray = array;
    }
    public int getId() {
      return id;
    }
    public void setId(int id) {
      this.id = id;
    }
    ...............
  }
```

> Eclipse provides a lot of helpful shortcuts but not for generating getter and setter methods. We can bind generating getter and setter methods to any key binding as per our liking. In Eclipse, go to **Window** | **Preferences** | **General** | **Keys**, search for getter, and add your bindings. We are using *Alt* + *Shift* + *G*; you are free to set any other key combination.

A database handler and queries

We will build our support class that will contain methods to read, update, and delete data as per our database requirements. This class will enable us to create and update the database and will act as our hub for data management. We will use this class to run SQLite queries and send across data to the UI; in our case, a listview to display the results:

```
public class DatabaseManager {

  private SQLiteDatabase db;
  private static final String DB_NAME = "contact";

  private static final int DB_VERSION = 1;
  private static final String TABLE_NAME = "contact_table";
  private static final String TABLE_ROW_ID = "_id";
  private static final String TABLE_ROW_NAME = "contact_name";
  private static final String TABLE_ROW_PHONENUM = "contact_number";
  private static final String TABLE_ROW_EMAIL = "contact_email";
  private static final String TABLE_ROW_PHOTOID = "photo_id";
  .........
}
```

We will create an object of the `SQLiteDatabase` class, which we will initialize later with either `getWritableDatabase()` or `getReadableDatabase()`. We will define the constants that we will be using through the class.

> By convention, constants are defined in capitals but use of `static final` in defining a constant is bit more than the convention. To know more, refer to `http://goo.gl/t0PoQj`.

We will define the name of our database as `contact` and define the version as 1. If we look back to the previous chapter, we will recall the importance of this value. A quick recap of this enables us to upgrade the database from the current version to the new version. The use case will become clear with this example. Let's say in future there is a new requirement, that is, we need to add a fax number to our contact details. We will modify our current schema to incorporate this change and our contact database will correspondingly change. If we are installing the application on new devices, there will be no issue; but in case of a device where we already have a running instance of the application, we will face problems. In this situation, `DB_VERSION` will come in handy and help us replace the old version of the database with the current version. Another approach would be to uninstall the application and install it again, but that is not encouraged.

The table name and important fields such as table columns will be defined now. `TABLE_ROW_ID` is a very important column. This will serve as the primary key for the table; it will also autoincrement and cannot be null. `NOT NULL` is again a column constraint, which may only be attached to a column definition and is not specified as a table constraint. Not surprisingly, a `NOT NULL` constraint dictates that the associated column may not contain a `NULL` value. Attempting to set the column value to `NULL` when inserting a new row or updating an existing one, causes a constraint violation. This will be used to find a particular value in the table. The uniqueness of the ID guarantees that we do not have any conflicts with data in the table, since each row is uniquely identified by the key. The rest of the table columns are pretty self-explanatory. The constructor for the `DatabaseManager` class is as follows:

```
public DatabaseManager(Context context) {
   this.context = context;
   CustomSQLiteOpenHelper helper = new CustomSQLiteOpenHelper(conte
xt);
   this.db = helper.getWritableDatabase();
  }
```

Notice that we are using a class called `CustomSQLiteOpenHelper`. We will come back to this later. We will use the class object to get our `SQLitedatabase` instance.

Building the Create query

To create a table with the desired columns, we will build a query statement and execute it. The statement will contain the table name, different table columns, and respective datatype. We will now look at methods for creating a new database and also upgrading an existing database according to the needs of the application:

```
private class CustomSQLiteOpenHelper extends SQLiteOpenHelper {
  public CustomSQLiteOpenHelper(Context context) {
    super(context, DB_NAME, null, DB_VERSION);
  }
  @Override
  public void onCreate(SQLiteDatabase db) {
String newTableQueryString = "create table "
+ TABLE_NAME + " ("
+ TABLE_ROW_ID
+ " integer primary key autoincrement not null,"
+ TABLE_ROW_NAME
+ " text not null,"
+ TABLE_ROW_PHONENUM
+ " text not null,"
+ TABLE_ROW_EMAIL
+ " text not null,"
+ TABLE_ROW_PHOTOID
+ " BLOB" + ");";
    db.execSQL(newTableQueryString);
  }

  @Override
  public void onUpgrade(SQLiteDatabase db, int oldVersion,
int newVersion) {

    String DROP_TABLE = "DROP TABLE IF EXISTS " +
TABLE_NAME;
    db.execSQL(DROP_TABLE);
    onCreate(db);
  }
}
```

`CustomSQLiteOpenHelper` extends `SQLiteOpenHelper` and provides us with the key methods `onCreate()` and `onUpgrade()`. We have defined this class as the inner class of our `DatabaseManager` class. This enables us to manage all the database-related functions, namely CRUD (Create,Read,Update, and Delete), from one place.

In our `CustomSQLiteOpenHelper` constructor, which is responsible for creating an instance of our class, we will pass a context, which in turn will be passed to the super constructor with the following parameters:

- `Context context`: This is the context we passed to our constructor
- `String name`: This is the name of our database
- `CursorFactory factory`: This is the cursor factory object, which can be passed as `null`
- `int version`: This is the database version of the database

The next important method is `onCreate()`. We will build our SQLite query string, which will create our database table:

```
"create table " + TABLE_NAME + " ("
+ TABLE_ROW_ID
+ " integer primary key autoincrement not null,"
.......
+ TABLE_ROW_PHOTOID + " BLOB" + ");";
```

The previous statement is based on the following syntax diagram:

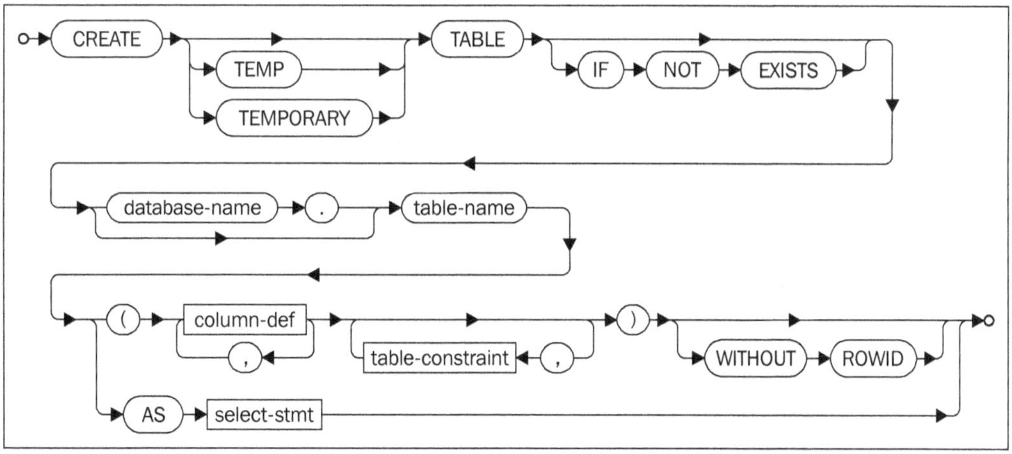

Here, the keyword `create table` is used to create a table. This is followed by the table name, the declaration of columns, and their datatype. After preparing our SQL statement, we will execute it using the `execSQL()` method of the SQLite database. In case something is wrong with the query statement that we built earlier, we will encounter the exception, `android.database.sqlite.SQLiteException`. By default, the database is formed in the internal memory space allocated to the application. The folder can be found at `/data/data/<yourpackage>/databases/`.

We can easily verify whether our database is formed while running this piece of code on an emulator or a rooted phone. In Eclipse, go to the DDMS perspective and then go to the file manager. We can easily navigate to the given folder if we have sufficient permission, that is, a rooted device. We can also pull up our database with the help of the file explorer, and with the help of a standalone SQLite manager tool, we can view our database and perform CRUD operations on it as well. What makes the Android application's database readable through another tool? Remember how we discussed cross-platform in SQLite features in the last chapter? In the following screenshot, notice the table name, the SQL statement used to build it, and the column names along with their datatype:

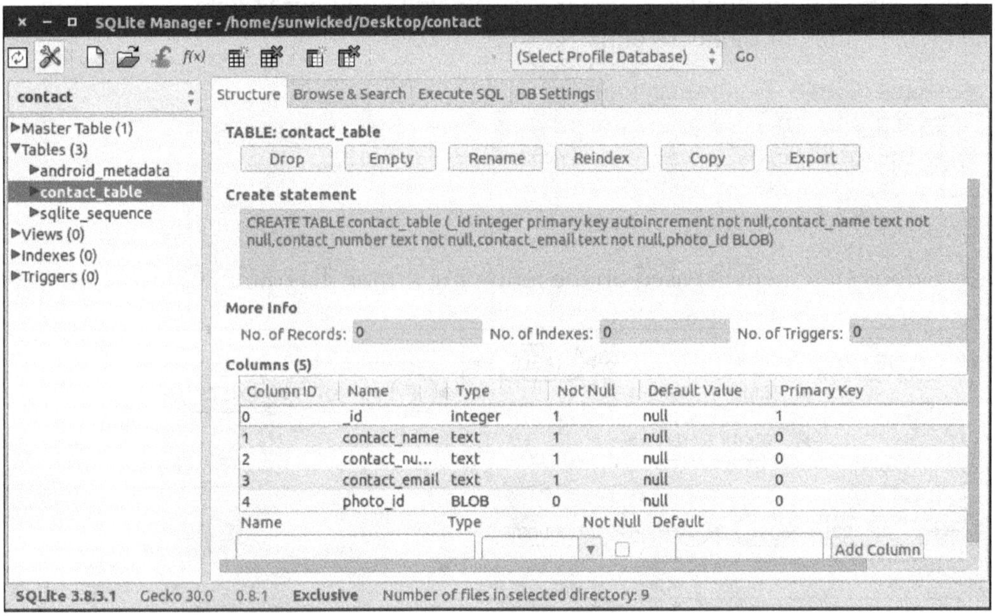

> The SQLite Manager tool can be downloaded either in the Chrome or Firefox browser. The following is the link for Firefox extension: `http://goo.gl/NLu8JT`.

Another handy way of pulling up our database or any other file is by using the `adb pull` command:

```
adb pull /data/data/your package name/databases  /file location
```

Another interesting point to note is that the datatype of `TABLE_ROW_PHOTOID` is `BLOB`. BLOB stands for binary large object. It is different from other datatype, such as text and integer, as it can store binary data. The binary data can be an image, audio, or any other type of multimedia object.

It is not advisable to store large images in a database; we can store filenames or locations, but storing images is bit of overkill. Imagine a situation like this where we store contact images. To amplify this situation, instead of a few hundred contacts, make it a few thousand contacts. The size of the database will become large and the access time will also increase. We want to demonstrate the use of BLOBs by storing contact images.

The `onUpgrade()` method is called when the database is upgraded. The database is upgraded by changing the version number of the database. Here, the implementation depends on the need of the application. In some cases, the whole table may have to be deleted and a new one may need to be created, and in some applications, only slight modification is needed. How to migrate from one version to another is covered in *Chapter 4, Thread Carefully*.

Building the Insert query

To insert a new row of data in the database table, we need to use either the `insert()` method or we can make an insert query statement and use the `execute()` method:

```
public void addRow(ContactModel contactObj) {
  ContentValues values = prepareData(contactObj);
  try {
    db.insert(TABLE_NAME, null, values);
  } catch (Exception e) {
    Log.e("DB ERROR", e.toString());
    e.printStackTrace();
  }
}
```

In case our table name is wrong, SQLite will give a log `no such table` message and the exception, `android.database.sqlite.SQLiteException`. The `addRow()` method is used to insert contact details in the database row; notice that the parameter of the method is an object of `ContactModel`. We have created an additional method `prepareData()` to construct a `ContentValues` object from the `ContactModel` object's getter methods:

```
.......................
values.put(TABLE_ROW_NAME, contactObj.getName());
values.put(TABLE_ROW_PHONENUM, contactObj.getContactNo());
....................
```

After the preparation of the `ContentValues` object, we are going to use the `insert()` method of the `SQLiteDatabase` class:

```
public long insert (String table, String nullColumnHack, ContentValues
values)
```

The parameters of the `insert()` method are as follows:

- `table`: The database table to insert the row into.
- `values`: This key-value map contains the initial column values for the table row. Column names act as keys. Values as the column values.
- `nullColumnHack`: This is as interesting as its name. Here's a quote from the Android documentation website:

"optional; may be null. SQL doesn't allow inserting a completely empty row without naming at least one column name. If your provided values are empty, no column names are known and an empty row can't be inserted. If not set to null, the nullColumnHack parameter provides the name of nullable column name to explicitly insert NULL into the case where your values are empty."

In short, in cases where we are trying to pass an empty `ContentValues` to be inserted, SQLite needs some column that is safe to be assigned `NULL`.

Alternatively, instead of the `insert()` method, we can prepare the SQL statement and execute it as shown:

```
public void addRowAlternative(ContactModel contactObj) {

  String insertStatment = "INSERT INTO " + TABLE_NAME
      + " ("
      + TABLE_ROW_NAME + ","
      + TABLE_ROW_PHONENUM + ","
      + TABLE_ROW_EMAIL + ","
      + TABLE_ROW_PHOTOID
      + ") "
      + " VALUES "
      + "(?,?,?,?)";

  SQLiteStatement s = db.compileStatement(insertStatment);
  s.bindString(1, contactObj.getName());
  s.bindString(2, contactObj.getContactNo());
  s.bindString(3, contactObj.getEmail());
if (contactObj.getPhoto() != null)
   {s.bindBlob(4, contactObj.getPhoto());}
  s.execute();
}
```

We will be covering alternatives for a lot of the methods we mentioned here. The idea is to make you comfortable with other possible ways to build and execute queries. The explanation of the alternative part is left as an exercise for you. The `getRowAsObject()` method will return the fetched row from the database in the form of a `ContactModel` object, as shown in the following code. It will require `rowID` as a parameter to uniquely identify which row in the table we want to access:

```
public ContactModel getRowAsObject(int rowID) {
  ContactModel rowContactObj = new ContactModel();
  Cursor cursor;
  try {
    cursor = db.query(TABLE_NAME, new String[] {
TABLE_ROW_ID, TABLE_ROW_NAME, TABLE_ROW_PHONENUM, TABLE_ROW_EMAIL,
TABLE_ROW_PHOTOID },
    TABLE_ROW_ID + "=" + rowID, null,
    null, null, null, null);
    cursor.moveToFirst();
    if (!cursor.isAfterLast()) {
      prepareSendObject(rowContactObj, cursor);     }
  } catch (SQLException e) {
      Log.e("DB ERROR", e.toString());
    e.printStackTrace();
  }
  return rowContactObj;
}
```

This method will return the fetched row from the database in the form of a `ContactModel` object. We are using the `SQLiteDatabase()` query method to fetch the row from our contact table against the provided `rowID` parameter. The method returns a cursor over the result set:

```
public Cursor query (String table, String[] columns, String selection,
String[] selectionArgs, String groupBy, String having, String orderBy,
String limit)
```

The following are the parameters of the previous code:

- `table`: This denotes the database table against which the query will be run.
- `columns`: This is a list of the columns that are returned; if we pass `null`, it will return all the columns.
- `selection`: This is where we define which rows are to be returned and framed as a SQL `WHERE` clause. Passing `null` will return all the rows.

- `selectionArgs`: We can pass `null` for this parameter or we may include question marks in the selection, which will be replaced by the values from `selectionArgs`.
- `groupBy`: This is a filter framed as a SQL `GROUP BY` clause declaring how to group rows. Passing `null` will cause the rows to not be grouped.
- `Having`: This is a filter that tells which row groups are to be made part of the cursor, framed as a SQL `HAVING` clause. Passing `null` will cause all the row groups to be included.
- `OrderBy`: This tells the query how to order the rows framed as an SQL `ORDER BY` clause. Passing `null` will use the default sort order.
- `limit`: This will limit the number of rows returned by the query framed as the `LIMIT` clause. Passing `null` denotes a no `LIMIT` clause.

Another important concept here is moving the cursor around to access data. Notice the following methods: `cursor.moveToFirst()`, `cursor.isAfterLast()`, and `cursor.moveToNext()`.

When we try to retrieve data-building SQL query statements, the database will first create an object of the cursor object and return its reference. The pointer of this returned reference is pointing to the 0th location, which is also known as "before first location" of the cursor. When we want to retrieve data, we have to first move to the first record; hence, the use of `cursor.moveToFirst()`.Talking about the rest of the two methods, `cursor.isAfterLast()` returns whether the cursor is pointing to the position after the last row and `cursor.moveToNext()` moves the cursor to the next row.

> Readers are advised to go through more of the cursor methods at the Android developer site: `http://goo.gl/fR75t8`.

Alternatively, we can use the following method:

```
public ContactModel getRowAsObjectAlternative(int rowID) {

  ContactModel rowContactObj = new ContactModel();
  Cursor cursor;

  try {
    String queryStatement = "SELECT * FROM "
       + TABLE_NAME  + " WHERE " + TABLE_ROW_ID + "=?";
```

```
        cursor = db.rawQuery(queryStatement,
          new String[]{String.valueOf(rowID)});
        cursor.moveToFirst();

        rowContactObj = new ContactModel();
        rowContactObj.setId(cursor.getInt(0));
        prepareSendObject(rowContactObj, cursor);

      } catch (SQLException e) {
        Log.e("DB ERROR", e.toString());
        e.printStackTrace();
      }

      return rowContactObj;
    }
```

The `update` statement is based on the following syntax diagram:

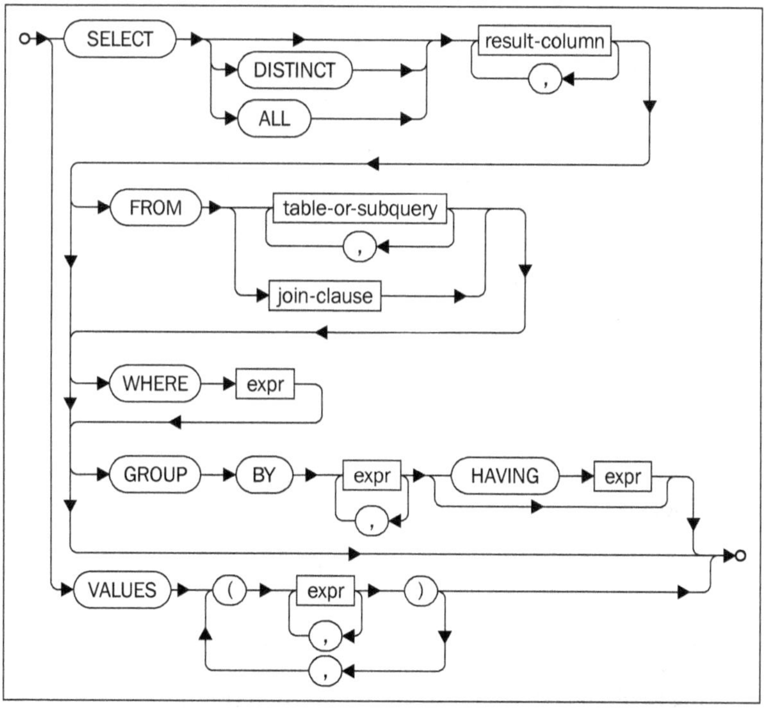

Before we move to other methods in the `datamanager` class, let's have a look at fetching data from a cursor object in the `prepareSendObject()` method:

```
rowObj.setContactNo(cursor.getString(cursor.
getColumnIndexOrThrow(TABLE_ROW_PHONENUM)));
rowObj.setEmail(cursor.getString(cursor.getColumnIndexOrThrow(TABLE_
ROW_EMAIL)));
```

Here `cursor.getstring()` takes the column index as a parameter and returns the value of the requested column, whereas `cursor.getColumnIndexOrThrow()` takes the column name as a parameter and returns the zero-based index for the given column name. Instead of this chaining approach, we can directly use `cursor.getstring()`. If we know the column number of the required column to fetch data from, we can use the following notation:

```
cursor.getstring(2);
```

Building the Delete query

To delete a particular row of data from our database table, we need to provide the primary key to uniquely identify the data set to be removed:

```
public void deleteRow(int rowID) {
  try {
    db.delete(TABLE_NAME, TABLE_ROW_ID
    + "=" + rowID, null);
  } catch (Exception e) {
    Log.e("DB ERROR", e.toString());
    e.printStackTrace();
  }
}
```

This method uses the SQLiteDatabase `delete()` method to delete the row of the given ID in the table:

```
public int delete (String table, String whereClause, String[]
whereArgs)
```

The following are the parameters of the preceding code snippet:

- `table`: This is the database table against which the query will be run
- `whereClause`: This is a clause to be applied when deleting a row; passing `null` in this clause will delete all the rows
- `whereArgs`: We may include question marks in the `where` clause, which will be replaced by the values that will be bound as strings

Alternatively, we can use the following method:

```
public void deleteRowAlternative(int rowId) {

  String deleteStatement = "DELETE FROM "
    + TABLE_NAME + " WHERE "
    + TABLE_ROW_ID + "=?";
  SQLiteStatement s = db.compileStatement(deleteStatement);
  s.bindLong(1, rowId);
  s.executeUpdateDelete();
}
```

The `delete` statement is based on the following syntax diagram:

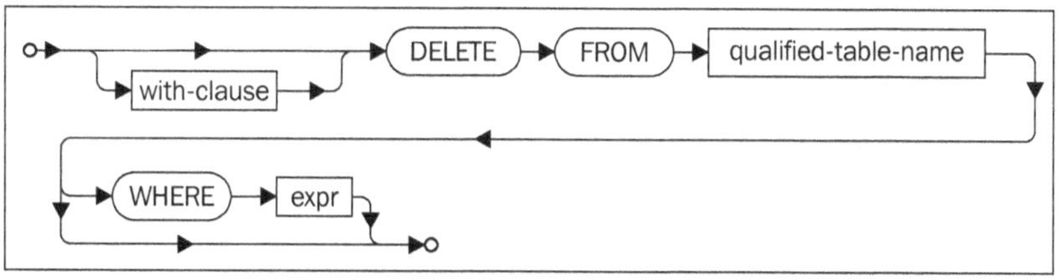

Building the Update query

To update an existing value, we need to use the `update()` method with the required parameters:

```
public void updateRow(int rowId, ContactModel contactObj) {

  ContentValues values = prepareData(contactObj);

  String whereClause = TABLE_ROW_ID + "=?";
  String whereArgs[] = new String[] {String.valueOf(rowId)};

  db.update(TABLE_NAME, values, whereClause, whereArgs);

}
```

Generally, we need the primary key, in our case the `rowId` parameter, to identify the row to be modified. An SQLiteDatabase `update()` method is used to modify the existing data of zero or more rows in a database table:

```
public int update (String table, ContentValues values, String
whereClause, String[] whereArgs)
```

The following are the parameters of the preceding code snippet:

- `table`: This is the qualified database table name to be updated.
- `values`: This is a mapping from the column names to the new column values.
- `whereClause`: This is the optional `WHERE` clause to be applied when updating a value/row. If the `UPDATE` statement does not have a `WHERE` clause, all the rows in the table are modified.
- `whereArgs`: We may include question marks in the `where` clause, which will be replaced by the values that will be bound as strings.

Alternatively, you can use the following code:

```
public void updateRowAlternative(int rowId, ContactModel contactObj) {
  String updateStatement = "UPDATE " + TABLE_NAME + " SET "
      + TABLE_ROW_NAME     + "=?,"
      + TABLE_ROW_PHONENUM + "=?,"
      + TABLE_ROW_EMAIL    + "=?,"
      + TABLE_ROW_PHOTOID  + "=?"
      + " WHERE " + TABLE_ROW_ID + "=?";

  SQLiteStatement s = db.compileStatement(updateStatement);
  s.bindString(1, contactObj.getName());
  s.bindString(2, contactObj.getContactNo());
  s.bindString(3, contactObj.getEmail());
  if (contactObj.getPhoto() != null)
   {s.bindBlob(4, contactObj.getPhoto());}
  s.bindLong(5, rowId);

  s.executeUpdateDelete();
}
```

The `update` statement is based on the following syntax diagram:

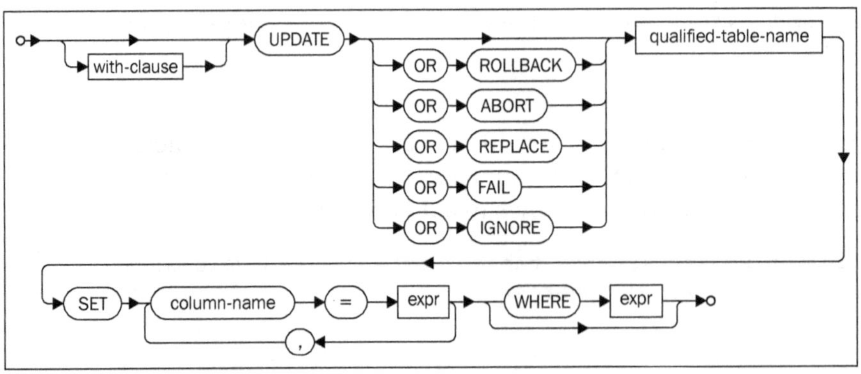

Connecting the UI and database

Now that we have our database hooks in place, let's connect our UI with the data:

1. The first step would be to get the data from the user. We can use the existing contact data from the Android's contact application by means of the content provider.

   We will be covering this approach in the next chapter. For now, we will be asking the user to add a new contact, which we will insert into the database:

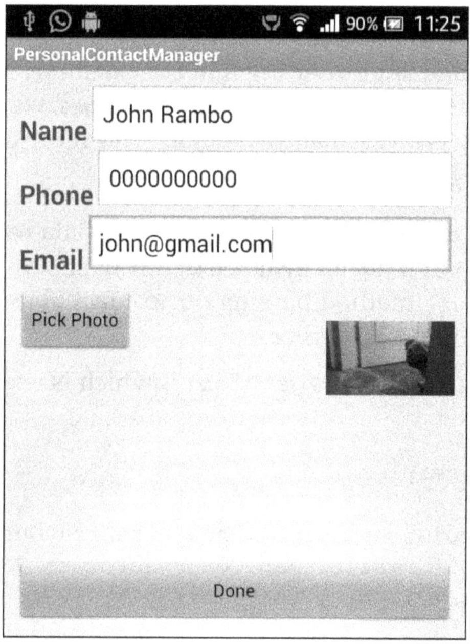

2. We are using standard Android UI widgets, such as `EditText`, `TextView`, and `Buttons` to collect the data provided by the user:

```
private void prepareSendData() {
  if (TextUtils.isEmpty(contactName.getText().toString())
      || TextUtils.isEmpty(
      contactPhone.getText().toString())) {

  .............

   } else {
    ContactModel contact = new ContactModel();
    contact.setName(contactName.getText().toString());
    ............

    DatabaseManager dm = new DatabaseManager(this);
```

```
        if(reqType == ContactsMainActivity
    .CONTACT_UPDATE_REQ_CODE) {
          dm.updateRowAlternative(rowId, contact);
        } else {
          dm.addRowAlternative(contact);
        }

        setResult(RESULT_OK);
        finish();
      }
    }
```

`prepareSendData()` is the method that is responsible for bundling data into our object model and later inserting it in our database. Notice that instead of using null check and length check on `contactName`, we are using `TextUtils.isEmpty()`, which is a very handy method. This returns `true` if the string is null or of zero length.

3. We prepare our `ContactModel` object from the data received by the user filling the form. We create an instance of our `DatabaseManager` class and access our `addRow()` method passing our contact object to be inserted in the database, as we discussed earlier.

   Another important method is `getBlob()`, which is used to get the image data in the BLOB format:

```
private byte[] getBlob() {

  ByteArrayOutputStream blob = new ByteArrayOutputStream();
  imageBitmap.compress(Bitmap.CompressFormat.JPEG, 100, blob);
  byte[] byteArray = blob.toByteArray();

  return byteArray;
}
```

4. We create a new `ByteArrayOutputStream` object `blob`. Bitmap's `compress()` method will be used to write a compressed version of the bitmap to our `outputstream` object:

```
public boolean compress (Bitmap.CompressFormat format, int
quality, OutputStream stream)
```

   The following are the parameters of the preceding code:

   - `format`: This is the format of a compressed image, in our case, JPEG.
   - `quality`: This is a hint to the compressor, which ranges from `0` to `100`. The value `0` means to compress to a smaller size and low quality, while `100` is for maximum quality.

  - `stream`: This is the output stream to write the compressed data to.

5. Then, we create our `byte[]` object, which will be constructed from the `ByteArrayOutputStream toByteArray()` method.

> You will notice that we are not covering all the methods; only those that are relevant to data operations and some methods or calls that might cause confusion. There are a few more methods that are used to invoke the camera or gallery to pick a photo to be used as the contact image. You are advised to explore the methods in the code provided along with the book.

Let's move on to the presentation part where we use a custom listview to display our contact information in a presentable and readable manner. We are going to skip a bulk of the code related to the presentation and concentrate on the parts where we fetch and provide data to our listview. We will also implement a context menu in order to provide a user with the functionality of deleting a particular contact. We will be touching base on the database manager methods such as `getAllData()` to fetch all our added contacts. We will use `deleteRow()` in order to remove any unwanted contacts from our contacts database. The final outcome will be something like the following screenshot:

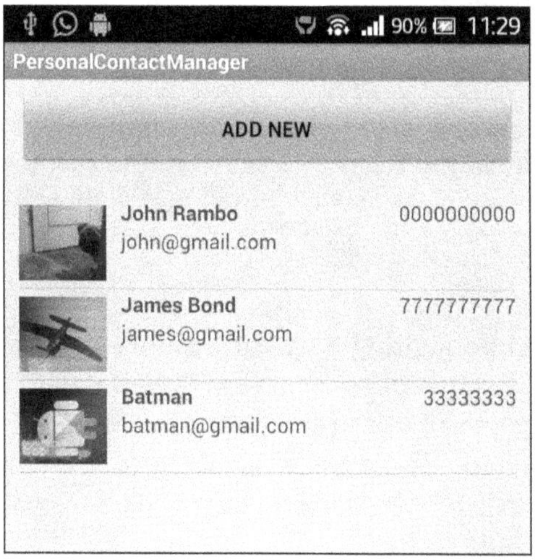

6. To make a custom listview similar to the one shown in the preceding screenshot, we create `CustomListAdapter` extending `BaseAdapter` and using the custom layout for the listview rows. Notice in the following constructor we have initialized a new array list and will use our database manager to fetch values by using the getAllData() method to fetch all the database entries:

```
public CustomListAdapter(Context context) {

    contactModelList = new ArrayList<ContactModel>();
    _context = context;
    inflater = (LayoutInflater)context.getSystemService(
Context.LAYOUT_INFLATER_SERVICE);
        dm = new DatabaseManager(_context);
    contactModelList = dm.getAllData();
}
```

   Another very important method is the `getView()` method. This is where we inflate our custom layout in a view:

```
convertView = inflater.inflate(R.layout.contact_list_row, null);
```

   We will use the view holder pattern to improve the listview scrolling smoothness:

```
vHolder = (ViewHolder) convertView.getTag();
```

7. And finally, set the data to the corresponding views:

```
vHolder.contact_email.setText(contactObj.getEmail());
```

> Holding view objects in a view holder improves the performance by reducing calls to `findViewById()`. You can read more about this and how to make listview scrolling smooth at `http://developer.android.com/training/improving-layouts/smooth-scrolling.html`.

8. We will also be implementing a way to delete a listview entry. We will use the context menu for this purpose. We will first create a menu item in the `menu` folder under `res` of our application structure:

```
<?xml version="1.0" encoding="utf-8"?>
<menu xmlns:android="http://schemas.android.com/apk/res/android" >

     <item
         android:id="@+id/delete_item"
         android:title="Delete"/>
<item
         android:id="@+id/update_item"
     android:title="Update"/>
</menu>
```

9. Now, in our main activity where we will display our listview, we will use the following call to register our listview with the context menu. In order to launch the context menu, we need to perform a long press action on the listview item:

   ```
   registerForContextMenu(listReminder)
   ```

10. There are a few more methods that we need to implement in order to achieve the delete functionality:

    ```
    @Override
      public void onCreateContextMenu(ContextMenu menu, View v,
          ContextMenuInfo menuInfo) {
        super.onCreateContextMenu(menu, v, menuInfo);
        MenuInflater m = getMenuInflater();
        m.inflate(R.menu.del_menu, menu);
      }
    ```

    This method is used to inflate the context menu with the menu we defined earlier in XML. The `MenuInfater` class generates menu objects from the menu XML files. Menu inflation relies heavily on the preprocessing of XML files that is done at build time; this is done to improve performance.

11. Now, we will implement a method to capture the click on the context menu:

    ```
      @Override
      public boolean onContextItemSelected(MenuItem item) {
    ..............
        case R.id.delete_item:

          cAdapter.delRow(info.position);
          cAdapter.notifyDataSetChanged();
          return true;
        case R.id.update_item:

          Intent intent = new Intent(
    ContactsMainActivity.this, AddNewContactActivity.class);
          ......................
      }
    ```

12. Here, we will find the position ID of the clicked listview item and invoke the `delRow()` method of the CustomListAdapter, and in the end, we will notify the adapter that the dataset has changed:

    ```
    public void delRow(int delPosition) {
                    dm.deleteRowAlternative(contactModelList.
    get(delPosition).getId());
           contactModelList.remove(delPosition);
    ```

The `delRow()` method is responsible for connecting our database's `deleteRowAlternative()` method to our context menu's `delete()` method. Here, we fetch the ID of the object set on the particular listview item and pass it to the `deleteRowAlternative()` method of `databaseManager` in order to delete the data from the database. After removing the data from the database, we will instruct our listview to remove the corresponding entry from our contact list.

In the `onContextItemSelected()` method, we can also see the `update_item` in case the user has clicked on the `update` button. We will launch the activity to add a new contact and add the data we already have in case the user wants to edit some fields. The catch is to know from where the call has been initiated. Is it to add a new entry or update an existing one? We take the help of the following code to tell the activity that this action is used to update rather than add a new entry:

```
intent.putExtra(REQ_TYPE, CONTACT_UPDATE_REQ_CODE);
```

Summary

In this chapter, we covered the steps of building up a database-based application, from scratch and then from schema to object model and then from object model to building actual databases. We underwent the process of building our database manager and finally implemented the UI database connect to achieve a fully functional application. The topics covered ranged from the building blocks of the model class, database schema to our database handler, and CRUD methods. We also covered the important concept of connecting a database to the Android views with proper hooks in place to pick up user data, add data to the database, and show relevant information after picking up data from the database.

In the next chapter, we will focus on building upon the groundwork we have done here. We will explore `ContentProviders`. We will also learn how to fetch data from `ContentProviders`, how to make our own content provider, the best practices associated while building them, and much more.

3
Sharing is Caring

"Data really powers everything that we do."

– Jeff Weiner, LinkedIn

In the last chapter, we started programming our very own contact manager. We came across various building blocks of a database-centric application; we covered database handlers and building queries in order to get meaningful data from our database. We also explored how to make a connection between our UI and database and present it in a consumable manner for the end user.

In this chapter, we will learn how to access other application's data via means of content providers. We will also learn how to build our very own content provider in order to share our data with other applications. We will look into Android's providers such as **contactprovider**. To wrap things up, we will construct a test application to use our newly constructed content provider.

In this chapter, we will cover the following topics:

- What is a content provider?
- Creating a content provider
- Implementing the core methods
- Using a content provider

What is a content provider?

A content provider is the fourth component of an Android application. It is used to manage access to a structured set of data. Content providers encapsulate the data, and provide abstraction and the mechanism to define data security. However, content providers are primarily intended to be used by other applications that access the provider using a provider's client object. Together, providers and provider clients offer a consistent, standard interface for data, which also handles interprocess communication and secure data access.

A content provider allows one app to share data with other applications. By design, an Android SQLite database created by an application is private to the application; it is excellent if you consider the security point of view, but troublesome when you want to share data across different applications. This is where a content provider comes to the rescue; you can easily share data by building your content provider. It is important to note that although our discussion will focus on a database, a content provider is not limited to it. It can also be used to serve file data that normally goes into files, such as photos, audio, or videos:

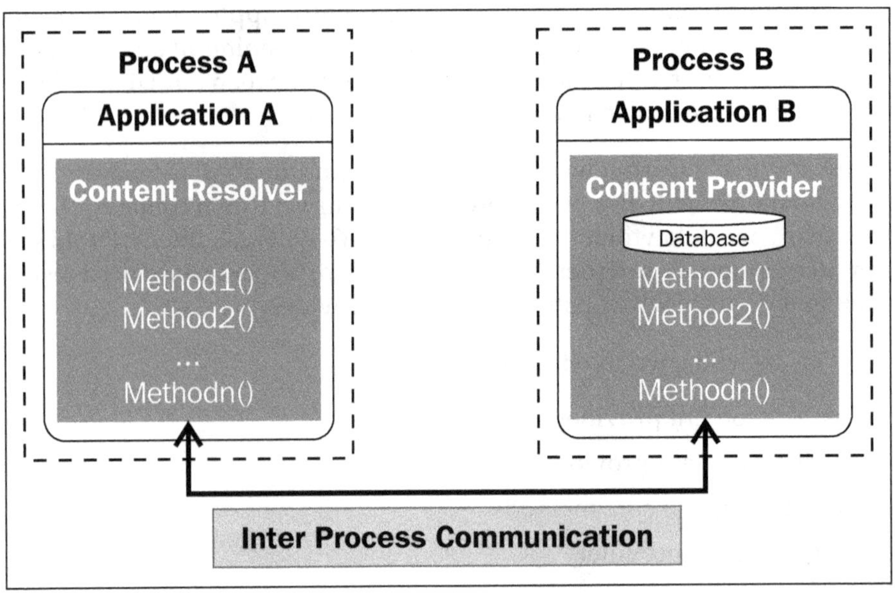

In the preceding diagram, notice how the interaction between Applications A and B happens while exchanging data. Here, we have an **Application A** whose activity needs to access the database of **Application B**. As we have already seen, the database of **Application B** is stored in the internal memory and cannot be directly accessed by **Application A**. This is where **Content Provider** comes into the picture; it allows us to share data and modify access to other applications. The content provider implements methods to query, insert, update, and delete data in databases. **Application A** now requests the content provider to perform some desired operations on behalf of it. We will explore both sides of the coin, but we will first use **Content Provider** to fetch contacts from a phone's contact database, and then we will build our very own content provider for others to pick data from our database.

Using existing content providers

Android lists a lot of standard content providers that we can use. Some of them are `Browser`, `CalendarContract`, `CallLog`, `Contacts`, `ContactsContract`, `MediaStore`, `userDictionary`, and so on.

In our current contact manager application, we will add a new feature. In the UI of the `AddNewContactActivity` class, we will add a small button to fetch contacts from a phone's contact list with help from the system's existing `ContentProvider` and `ContentResolver` providers. We will be using the `ContactsContract` provider for this purpose.

What is a content resolver?

The `ContentResolver` object in the application's context is used to communicate with the provider as a client. The `ContentResolver` object communicates with the provider object—an instance of a class that implements `ContentProvider`. The provider object receives data requests from clients, performs the requested action, and returns the results.

ContentResolver is a single, global instance in our application that provides access to other application's content providers; we do not need to worry about handling interprocess communication. The ContentResolver methods provide the basic CRUD (create, retrieve, update, and delete) functions of persistent storage; it has methods that call identically named methods in the provider object but does not know the implementation. We will cover ContentResolver in more detail as we progress through this chapter.

In the preceding screenshot, notice the new icon on the right-hand side to add contacts directly from the phone contacts; we modified the existing XML to add the icon. The corresponding class AddNewContactActivity will also be modified:

```
public void pickContact() {
    try {
        Intent cIntent = new Intent(Intent.ACTION_PICK,
              ContactsContract.Contacts.CONTENT_URI);
      startActivityForResult(cIntent, PICK_CONTACT);
    } catch (Exception e) {
      e.printStackTrace();
      Log.i(TAG, "Exception while picking contact");
    }
  }
```

We added a new method pickContact() to prepare an intent in order to pick contacts. Intent.ACTION_PICK allows us to pick an item from a data source; in addition, all we need to know is the **Uniform Resource Identifier** (**URI**) of the provider, which in our case is ContactsContract.Contacts.CONTENT_URI. This functionality is also provided by Messaging, Gallery, and Contacts. If you look into the code from *Chapter 2, Connecting the Dots*, you will find we have used the same code to pick images from Gallery. The Contacts screen will pop up allowing us to browse or search for contacts we require to migrate to our new application. Notice onActivityResult, that is, our next stop we will modify this method to handle our corresponding request to handle contacts. Let us look at the code we have to add to pick contacts from an Android's contact provider:

```
{
.
.
.

else if (requestCode == PICK_CONTACT) {
      if (resultCode == Activity.RESULT_OK)

       {
          Uri contactData = data.getData();
          Cursor c = getContentResolver().query(contactData, null,
null, null, null);
         if (c.moveToFirst()) {
             String id = c
                   .getString(c
                         .getColumnIndexOrThrow(ContactsContract.
Contacts._ID));

             String hasPhone = c
                   .getString(c
                         .getColumnIndex(ContactsContract.Contacts.
HAS_PHONE_NUMBER));

            if (hasPhone.equalsIgnoreCase("1")) {
                Cursor phones = getContentResolver()
                      .query(ContactsContract.CommonDataKinds.Phone.
CONTENT_URI,
                           null,
                           ContactsContract.CommonDataKinds.Phone.
CONTACT_ID
                                  + " = " + id, null, null);
               phones.moveToFirst();
               contactPhone.setText(phones.getString(phones
                      .getColumnIndex("data1")));

               contactName
                      .setText(phones.getString(phones
                            .getColumnIndex(ContactsContract.Contacts.
DISPLAY_NAME)));

 }
.....
```

> To add a little flair to your application, download the entire set of stencils, sources, the action bar icon pack, color swatches, and the Roboto font family from the Android developer site, `http://goo.gl/4Msuct`. Designing a functional application is incomplete without a consistent UI that follows Android guidelines.

We start by checking whether the request code matches ours. Then, we cross-check `resultcode`. We get the `ContentResolver` object by making a call to `getcontentresolver` on the `Context` object; it is a method of the `android.content.Context` class. As we are in an activity that inherits from `Context`, we do not need to be explicit in making a call to it. The same goes for services. We will now verify whether the contact we picked has a phone number or not. After verifying the necessary details, we pull the data that we require, such as contact name and phone number, and set them in relevant fields.

Creating a content provider

A content provider provides access to data in two ways: one is structured data that goes in the form of a database, as the example we are working on currently, or in the form of file data, that is, data that goes in the form of pictures, audio, video, and so on stored in the private space of the application. Before we begin digging into how to create a content provider, we should also retrospect whether we need one. If we want to offer data to other applications, allow users to copy data from our app to another, or use the search framework in our application, then the answer is yes.

Just like other Android components (`Activity`, `Service`, or `BroadcastReceiver`), a content provider is created by extending the `ContentProvider` class. Since `ContentProvider` is an abstract class, we have to implement the six abstract methods. These methods are as follows:

Method	Usage
`void onCreate()`	Initializes the provider
`String getType(Uri)`	Returns the MIME type of data in the content provider
`int delete(Uri uri, String selection, String[] selectionArgs)`	Deletes data from the content provider

Method	Usage
`Uri insert(Uri uri, ContentValues values)`	Inserts new data into the content provider
`Cursor query(Uri uri, String[] projection, String selection, String[] selectionArgs, String sortOrder)`	Returns data to the caller
`int update(Uri uri, ContentValues values, String selection, String[] selectionArgs)`	Updates the existing data in the content provider

These methods will be dealt with in more detail later as we progress through the chapter and build our application.

Understanding content URIs

Every data access method of `ContentProvider` has a content URI, as an argument that allows it to determine the table, row, or file to access. It generally follows the following structure:

```
content://authority/Path/Id
```

Let's analyze the breakdown of the components of the `content://` URI. The scheme for content providers is always `content`. The colon and double-slash (`://`) act as a separator from the authority part. Then, we have the `authority` part. By rule, authorities have to be unique for every content provider. The naming convention the Android documentation recommends using is the fully qualified class name of your content provider subclass. Generally, it is built as a package name plus a qualifier for each content provider we publish.

The remaining part is optional, also referred to as **path**, and is used for segregation between different types of data our content provider can provide. A very good example is the `MediaStore` provider which needs to distinguish between audio, video, and image files.

Another optional part is `id`, which points to a specific record; depending on whether `id` is present or not, the URI becomes ID-based or directory-based, respectively. Another way to understand it would be that an ID-based URI enables us to interact with data individually at row level, whereas a directory-based URI enables us to interact with multiple rows of a database.

For example, consider `content://com.personalcontactmanager.provider/contacts`; we will encounter this soon enough as we move ahead with the chapter where we define how to access the content provider we are currently building.

> On a side note, the package name for applications should always be unique; this is because all the applications on Play Store are identified by their package name. All the updates for an application on Play Store need to have the same package name and be signed with the same keystore used initially. For instance, the following is the Play Store link of a Gmail application; notice that at the end of URL, we will find the package name of the application:
>
> `play.google.com/store/apps/details?id=com.google.android.gm`

Declaring our contract class

Declaring a contract is a very important part of building our content provider. This class, as the name suggests, will act as a contract between our content provider and the application that is going to access our content provider. It is a `public final` class, which contains constant definitions for URIs, column names, and other metadata. It can also contain Javadoc, but the biggest advantage is that the developer using it need not worry about the names of tables, columns, and constants, leading to less error-prone code.

The contract class provides us with the necessary abstraction; we can change the underlying operations as and when required and we can also change the corresponding data manipulation affecting other dependent applications. An important thing to note is that we need to be careful while changing the contract in future; if we are not careful, we might break the other applications that are using our contract class.

Our contract class looks like the following:

```
public final class PersonalContactContract {

    /**
     * The authority of the PersonalContactProvider
     */
    public static final String AUTHORITY = "com.personalcontactmanager.
provider";

    public static final String BASE_PATH = "contacts";

    /**
```

```
     * The Uri for the top-level PersonalContactProvider
     * authority
     */
    public static final Uri CONTENT_URI = Uri.parse("content://" +
AUTHORITY
          + "/" + BASE_PATH);

    /**
     * The mime type of a directory of items.
     */
    public static final String CONTENT_TYPE =
ContentResolver.CURSOR_DIR_BASE_TYPE +
                  "/vnd.com.personalcontactmanager.provider.table";
    /**
     * The mime type of a single item.
     */
    public static final String CONTENT_ITEM_TYPE =
ContentResolver.CURSOR_ITEM_BASE_TYPE +
                 "/vnd.com.personalcontactmanager.provider.table_
item";

    /**
     * A projection of all columns
     * in the items table.
     */
    public static final String[] PROJECTION_ALL = { "_id",
       "contact_name", "contact_number",
       "contact_email", "photo_id" };

    /**
     * The default sort order for
     * queries containing NAME fields.
     */
    //public static final String SORT_ORDER_DEFAULT = NAME + " ASC";

    public static final class Columns {
       public static String TABLE_ROW_ID = "_id";
       public static String TABLE_ROW_NAME  = "contact_name";
       public static String TABLE_ROW_PHONENUM = "contact_number";
       public static String TABLE_ROW_EMAIL = "contact_email";
       public static String TABLE_ROW_PHOTOID = "photo_id";
    }
}
```

`AUTHORITY` is the symbolic name that identifies the provider among many other providers registered as part of an Android system. `BASE_PATH` is the path of the table. `CONTENT_URI` is the URI of the table encapsulated by the provider. `CONTENT_TYPE` is the Android platform's base MIME type for content URI containing a cursor of zero or more items. `CONTENT_ITEM_TYPE` is the Android platform's base MIME type for content URIs containing a cursor of a single item. `PROJECTION_ALL` and `Columns` contain the column IDs of the table.

Without this information, other developers will not be able to access your provider even though it is open for access.

> There can be many tables inside a provider and each should have a unique path; the path is not a real physical path but an identifier.

Creating UriMatcher definitions

`UriMatcher` is a utility class, which aids in matching URIs in content providers. The `addURI()` method takes the content URI patterns that the provider should recognize. We add a URI to match, and the code to return when this URI is matched:

```
addURI(String authority, String path, int code)
```

We pass `authority`, a `path` pattern, and an integer value to the `addURI()` method of `UriMatcher`; it returns the `int` value, which we defined as constant when we tried to match patterns.

Our `UriMatcher` looks like the following:

```
private static final int CONTACTS_TABLE = 1;
private static final int CONTACTS_TABLE_ITEM = 2;

private static final UriMatcher mmURIMatcher = new
UriMatcher(UriMatcher.NO_MATCH);
   static {
      mmURIMatcher.addURI(PersonalContactContract.AUTHORITY,
            PersonalContactContract.BASE_PATH, CONTACTS_TABLE);
      mmURIMatcher.addURI(PersonalContactContract.AUTHORITY,
            PersonalContactContract.BASE_PATH+  "/#",
                       CONTACTS_TABLE_ITEM);
   }
```

Notice that it also supports the use of wildcards; we have used hashtag (#) in the preceding code snippet, we can also use wildcards such as `*`. In our case, with the hashtag, `" content://com.personalcontactmanager.provider/contacts/2"` this expression matches, but using `* "content://com.personalcontactmanager.provider/contacts` it doesn't.

Implementing the core methods

In order to build our content provider, the next step will be to prepare our core database access and data modifying methods, better known as CRUD methods. This is where the core logic of how we want to interact with our data depending on the insert, query, or delete calls received is specified. We will also implement the Android architecture's life cycle methods such as `onCreate()`.

Initializing the provider through the onCreate() method

We create an object of our database manager class in `onCreate()`. There should be minimum operations in `oncreate()` as it runs on the Main UI thread, and it may cause lag for some users. It is good practice to avoid long-running tasks in `oncreate()` as it increases the startup time of the provider. It is even recommended to defer database creation and data loading until our provider actually receives a request for the data, that is, to move long-lasting actions to the CRUD methods:

```
@Override
Public Boolean onCreate() {
   dbm = new DatabaseManager(getContext());
   return false;
}
```

Querying records through the query() method

The `query()` method will return a cursor over the result set. The URI is passed to our `UriMatcher` to see whether it matches any patterns we defined earlier. In our switch case statement, if it is a table-item-related case, we check whether the `selection` statement is empty; in case it is, we build our selection statement up to the `lastpathsegment`, else we append the selection to the `lastpathsegment` statement. We use a `DatabaseManager` object to a run query on the database and get a cursor as a result. It is expected of the `query()` method to throw an `IllegalArgumentException` to inform of an unknown URI; it is also good practice to throw a `nullPointerException` in case we encounter an internal error during the query process:

```
@Override
public Cursor query(Uri uri, String[] projection, String selection,
      String[] selectionArgs, String sortOrder) {

   int uriType = mmURIMatcher.match(uri);
```

```
    switch(uriType) {

    case CONTACTS_TABLE:
       break;
    case CONTACTS_TABLE_ITEM:
       if (TextUtils.isEmpty(selection)) {
          selection = PersonalContactContract.Columns.TABLE_ROW_ID
                  + "=" + uri.getLastPathSegment();
       } else {
          selection = PersonalContactContract.Columns.TABLE_ROW_ID
                  + "=" + uri.getLastPathSegment() +
                " and " + selection;
       }
       break;
    default:
       throw new IllegalArgumentException("Unknown URI: " + uri);
    }

    Cursor cr = dbm.getRowAsCursor(projection, selection,
                selectionArgs, sortOrder);

    return cr;
 }
```

> Remember that an Android system must be able to communicate the exception across process boundaries. Android can do this for the following exceptions that may be useful in handling query errors:
>
> - `IllegalArgumentException`: You may choose to throw this if your provider receives an invalid content URI
> - `NullPointerException`: This is thrown when the object is null and we try to access its field or method

Adding records through the insert() method

As the name suggests, the `insert()` method is used to insert a value in our database. It returns the URI of the inserted row and, while checking the URI, we need to remember that an insertion can happen at the table level, hence the operations in the method are processed at the URI that matches the table. After matching, we use the standard `DatabaseManager` object to insert our new value into the database. The content URI for the new row is constructed by appending the new row's `_ID` value to the table's content URI:

```
@Override
public Uri insert(Uri uri, ContentValues values) {

    int uriType = mmURIMatcher.match(uri);
    long id;

    switch(uriType) {
    case CONTACTS_TABLE:
        id = dbm.addRow(values);
        break;
    default:
        throw new IllegalArgumentException("Unknown URI: " + uri);
    }

    Uri ur = ContentUris.withAppendedId(uri, id);
    return ur;
}
```

Updating records through the update() method

The `update()` method updates an existing row in the appropriate table, using the values in the `ContentValues` argument. First, we identify the URI, whether it is directory-based or ID-based, then we build our selection statement as we did in the `query()` method. Now, we will execute the standard `updateRow()` method of `DatabaseManager` that we defined earlier while building this application in *Chapter 2, Connecting the Dots*, which returns the number of affected rows.

The `update()` method returns the number of rows updated. Based on the selection clause, one or more rows can be updated:

```
@Override
public int update(Uri uri, ContentValues values, String selection,
      String[] selectionArgs) {
```

```
    int uriType = mmURIMatcher.match(uri);

    switch(uriType) {
    case CONTACTS_TABLE:
       break;
    case CONTACTS_TABLE_ITEM:
       if (TextUtils.isEmpty(selection)) {
          selection = PersonalContactContract.Columns.TABLE_ROW_ID
 + "=" + uri.getLastPathSegment();
       } else {
          selection = PersonalContactContract.Columns.TABLE_ROW_ID
+ "=" + uri.getLastPathSegment()
+ " and " + selection;
       }
       break;
    default:
       throw new IllegalArgumentException("Unknown URI: " + uri);
    }

    int count = dbm.updateRow(values, selection, selectionArgs);

    return count;
}
```

Deleting records through the delete() method

The `delete()` method is very similar to the `update()` method and the process of using it is similar; here, the call is made to delete a row instead of updating it. The `delete()` method returns the number of rows deleted. Based on the selection clause, one or more rows can be deleted:

```
@Override
public int delete(Uri uri, String selection, String[] selectionArgs) {

    int uriType = mmURIMatcher.match(uri);

    switch(uriType) {
    case CONTACTS_TABLE:
       break;
    case CONTACTS_TABLE_ITEM:
       if (TextUtils.isEmpty(selection)) {
          selection = PersonalContactContract.Columns.TABLE_ROW_ID
 + "=" + uri.getLastPathSegment();
       } else {
```

```
            selection = PersonalContactContract.Columns.TABLE_ROW_ID
    + "=" + uri.getLastPathSegment()
    + " and " + selection;
        }
        break;
    default:
        throw new IllegalArgumentException("Unknown URI: " + uri);
    }

    int count = dbm.deleteRow(selection, selectionArgs);

    return count;
}
```

Getting the return type of data through the getType() method

The signature of this simple method takes a URI and returns a string value; every content provider must return the content type for its supported URIs. A very interesting fact is that no permissions are needed for an application to access this information; if our content provider requires permissions, or is not exported, all the applications can still call this method regardless of their access permissions to retrieve MIME types.

All these MIME types should be declared in the contract class:

```
@Override
public String getType(Uri uri) {

    int uriType = mmURIMatcher.match(uri);
    switch(uriType) {
    case CONTACTS_TABLE:
        return PersonalContactContract.CONTENT_TYPE;
    case CONTACTS_TABLE_ITEM:
        return PersonalContactContract.CONTENT_ITEM_TYPE;
    default:
        throw new IllegalArgumentException("Unknown URI: " + uri);
    }

}
```

Adding a provider to a manifest

Another important step is to add our content provider to a manifest, like we do with other Android components. We can register multiple providers here. The important bit here, other than `android:authorities`, is `android:exported`; it defines whether the content provider is available for other applications to use. In case of `true`, the provider is available to other applications; if it is `false`, the provider is not available to other applications. If applications have the same user ID (UID) as the provider, they will have access to it:

```
<provider
   android:name="com.personalcontactmanager.provider.
PersonalContactProvider"
   android:authorities="com.personalcontactmanager.provider"
   android:exported="true"
   android:grantUriPermissions="true" >
   </provider>
```

Another important concept is **permissions**. We can add additional security by adding read and write permissions, which the other application has to add in their manifest XML file and, in turn, automatically inform a user that they are going to use a particular application's content provider either to read, write, or both. We can add permissions in the following manner:

```
android:readPermission="com.personalcontactmanager.provider.READ"
```

Using a content provider

The main reason we built a content provider was to allow other applications to access the complex data store in our database and perform CRUD operations. We will now build one more application in order to test our newly built content provider. The test application is very simple, comprising of only one activity class and one layout file. It has standard buttons to perform actions. Nothing fancy, just the tools for us to test the functionality we just implemented. We will now delve into the `TestMainActivity` class and look into its implementation:

```
public class TestMainActivity extends Activity {


public final String AUTHORITY = "com.personalcontactmanager.provider";
public final String BASE_PATH = "contacts";
private TextViewqueryT, insertT;

public class Columns {
```

```
    public final static String TABLE_ROW_ID = "_id";
    public final static String TABLE_ROW_NAME = "contact_name";
    public final static String TABLE_ROW_PHONENUM =

"contact_number";
    public final static String TABLE_ROW_EMAIL = "contact_email";
    public final static String TABLE_ROW_PHOTOID = "photo_id";
    }
```

To access a content provider, we need details such as `AUTHORITY` and `BASE_PATH` and the names of the columns of database tables; we need to access the public class `Columns` for this purpose. We have more tables and we will see more of these classes. Generally, all this necessary information will be taken from the published contract class of the content provider. Some content providers also require implementing read or write permissions in the manifest:

```
<uses-permissionandroid:name="AUTHORITY.permission.WRITE_TASKS"/>
```

In some cases, the content provider we need to access can ask us to add permissions in our manifest. When the users install the application, they will see an added permission in their permission list:

```
@Override
protected void onCreate(Bundle savedInstanceState) {
    super.onCreate(savedInstanceState);
    setContentView(R.layout.activity_test_main);
    queryT = (TextView) findViewById(R.id.textQuery);
    insertT = (TextView) findViewById(R.id.textInsert);
    }
```

> To try out some other app's content provider, refer to `http://goo.gl/NEX2hN`.
>
> It lists how you can use the Any.do's content provider—a very famous task application.

We will set our layout and initialize the views we require in `onCreate()` of activity. To query, we first need to prepare the URI object that matches the table.

Content resolver now comes into play; it acts as a resolver for the content URI we prepared. Our `getContentResolver.query()` method, in this case, will fetch all the columns and rows. We will now move the cursor to the first position in order to read the result. For testing purposes, it's read as a string:

```
public void query(View v) {
```

```
    Uri contentUri = Uri.parse("content://" + AUTHORITY
                + "/" + BASE_PATH);

    Cursor cr = getContentResolver().query(contentUri, null,
              null, null, null);

    if (cr != null) {
        if (cr.getCount() > 0) {
           cr.moveToFirst();
           String name = cr.getString(cr.getColumnIndexOrThrow(
  Columns.TABLE_ROW_NAME));
           queryT.setText(name);
        }
    }

    ....
    ....
  }
```

Now, we build a URI to read a particular row instead of a complete table. We already mentioned that to make URI ID-based, we need to add the ID part to our existing `contenturi`. Now, we build our projection string array to be passed as a parameter in our `query()` method:

```
  public void query(View v) {

    ...
    ...

    Uri rowUri = contentUri = ContentUris.withAppendedId
              (contentUri, getFirstRowId());

    String[] projection = new String[] {
        Columns.TABLE_ROW_NAME, Columns.TABLE_ROW_PHONENUM,
        Columns.TABLE_ROW_EMAIL, Columns.TABLE_ROW_PHOTOID };

    cr = getContentResolver().query(contentUri, projection,
        null, null, null);

    if (cr != null) {
        if (cr.getCount() > 0) {
           cr.moveToFirst();
           String name = cr.getString(cr.getColumnIndexOrThrow(
                  Columns.TABLE_ROW_NAME));
```

```
            queryT.setText(name);

        }
    }

}
```

The `getFirstRowId()` method gets the ID of the first row in the table. It is done because the ID of the first row will not always be `1`. It changes when the rows are deleted. If the first item in the table with row ID `1` is deleted, then the second item with row ID `1` becomes the first item:

```
private int getFirstRowId() {

  int id = 1;
  Uri contentUri = Uri.parse("content://" + AUTHORITY + "/"
             + "contacts");
  Cursor cr = getContentResolver().query(contentUri, null,
            null, null, null);
  if (cr != null) {
      if (cr.getCount() > 0) {
         cr.moveToFirst();
         id = cr.getInt(cr.getColumnIndexOrThrow(
            Columns.TABLE_ROW_ID));
      }
  }
return id;

}
```

Let's take a closer look at the `query()` method:

```
public final Cursor query (Uri uri, String[] projection, String
selection, String[] selectionArgs, String sortOrder)
```

Present in API level 1, the `query()` method returns a cursor over the result set against the parameters we supplied. The following are the parameters of the preceding code:

- `uri`: This is `contentURI` in our case, using the `content://` scheme for the content to be retrieved. It can be ID-based or directory-based.
- `projection`: This is a list of the columns to be returned as we have prepared using the column names. Passing `null` will return all the columns.
- `selection`: Formatted as a SQL `WHERE` clause, excluding the `WHERE` itself, this acts as a filter declaring which rows to return.

- `selectionArgs`: We may include `?` parameter markers in `selection`. Android SQL query builder will replace the `?` parameter markers by the values bound as string from `selectionArgs`, in the order that they appear in the `selection`.
- `sortOrder`: This tells us how to order the rows, formatted as an SQL `ORDER BY` clause. A `null` value will use the default sort order.

> According to official documentation, there are a few guidelines we should follow for optimum performance:
>
> - Provide an explicit projection to prevent reading data from storage that isn't going to be used.
> - Use question mark parameter markers such as `phone=?` instead of explicit values in the selection parameter, so that queries that differ only by those values will be recognized as the same for caching purposes.

The same process we used earlier to check for `null` values and an empty cursor is performed, and finally, a required value is extracted from the cursor.

Now, let us look at the `insert` method for our test application.

We start by building our content value object and relevant key-value pairs, for instance, putting a phone number in the relevant `Columns.TABLE_ROW_PHONENUM` field. Notice that because details such as a column's name were shared with us in the form of a class, we need not worry about details such as the actual column name. We just need to access it via means of the `Columns` class. This ensures that we only need to update the relevant values. If in future the content provider undergoes some change and changes the table names, the rest of the functionality and implementation remains the same. We build our projection string array with the column names we required, as we did earlier in the case of querying the content provider for data.

We also build our content URI; notice that it matches the table and not individual rows. The `insert()` method also returns a URI unlike the `query()` method, which returned a cursor over the result set:

```
public void insert(View v) {

  String name = getRandomName();
  String number = getRandomNumber();

  ContentValues values = new ContentValues();
  values.put(Columns.TABLE_ROW_NAME, name);
  values.put(Columns.TABLE_ROW_PHONENUM, number);
  values.put(Columns.TABLE_ROW_EMAIL, name + "@gmail.com");
  values.put(Columns.TABLE_ROW_PHOTOID, "abc");
```

```
    String[] projection = new String[] {
        Columns.TABLE_ROW_NAME, Columns.TABLE_ROW_PHONENUM,
        Columns.TABLE_ROW_EMAIL, Columns.TABLE_ROW_PHOTOID };

    Uri contentUri = Uri.parse("content://" + AUTHORITY + "/"
            + BASE_PATH);

    Uri insertedRowUri = getContentResolver().insert(
            contentUri, values);

    //checking the added row
    Cursor cr = getContentResolver().query(insertedRowUri,
          projection, null, null, null);

    if (cr != null) {
        if (cr.getCount() > 0) {
            cr.moveToFirst();
            name = cr.getString(cr.getColumnIndexOrThrow(
                Columns.TABLE_ROW_NAME));
            insertT.setText(name);
        }
    }

}
```

The `getRandomName()` and `getRandomNumber()` methods generate a random name and number to insert in the table:

```
private String getRandomName() {

      Random rand = new Random();
      String name = "" + (char) (122-rand.nextInt(26))
         + (char) (122-rand.nextInt(26))
         + (char) (122-rand.nextInt(26))
         + (char) (122-rand.nextInt(26))
         + (char) (122-rand.nextInt(26))
         + (char) (122-rand.nextInt(26))
         + (char) (122-rand.nextInt(26))
         + (char) (122-rand.nextInt(26)) ;

      return name;
}

public String getRandomNumber() {
```

```
        Random rand = new Random();
        String number = rand.nextInt(98989)*rand.nextInt(59595)+"";

        return number;
    }
```

Let's take a closer look at the `insert()` method:

```
public final Uri insert (Uri url, ContentValues values)
```

The following are the parameters of the preceding line of code:

- `url`: The URL of the table to insert the data into
- `values`: The values for the newly inserted row in the form of a `ContentValues` object, the key is the column name for the field

Notice that after inserting, we are running the `query()` method again with the URI that was returned by the `insert()` method. We run this to see that the value we intended to insert has been inserted; this query will return columns as per the projection of the row whose ID is appended.

So far, we have covered the `query()` and `insert()` methods; now, we will cover the `update()` method.

We progressed in the `insert()` method by preparing the `ContentValues` object. Similarly, we will prepare an object that we will use in the `update()` method of `ContentResolver` to update an existing row. We will build our URI in this case up to the ID, as this operation is ID based. Update the row as pointed by the `rowUri` object and it will return the number of rows updated, which will be the same as the URI; in this case, it is `rowUri` that points to only a single row. An alternate method could be using a combination of `contentUri` (which points to the table) and `selection`/`selectionArgs`. In this case, the rows updated could be more than one as per the `selection` clause:

```
public void update(View v) {

    String name = getRandomName();
    String number = getRandomNumber();

    ContentValues values = new ContentValues();
    values.put(Columns.TABLE_ROW_NAME, name);
    values.put(Columns.TABLE_ROW_PHONENUM, number);
    values.put(Columns.TABLE_ROW_EMAIL, name + "@gmail.com");
    values.put(Columns.TABLE_ROW_PHOTOID, " ");

    Uri contentUri = Uri.parse("content://" + AUTHORITY
                    + "/" + BASE_PATH);
```

```
    Uri rowUri = ContentUris.withAppendedId(
                    contentUri, getFirstRowId());
    int count = getContentResolver().update(rowUri, values, null, null);

}
```

Let's take a closer look at the `update()` method:

```
public final int update (Uri uri, ContentValues values, String where,
String[] selectionArgs)
```

The following are the parameters of the preceding line of code:

- `uri`: This is the content URI we wish to modify
- `values`: This is similar to the values we used earlier with other methods; passing a `null` value will remove an existing field value
- `where`: A SQL `WHERE` clause that acts as a filter to rows before updating them

We can run the `query()` method again to see whether the change is reflected; this activity has been left as an exercise for you.

The last method is `delete()`, which we require in order to complete our arsenal of CRUD methods. The `delete()` method begins in a similar fashion as the rest of the methods do; first, prepare our content URI at the directory level and then build it for the ID level, that is, at the individual row level. After that, we pass it to the `delete()` method of `ContentResolver`. Unlike the `query()` and `insert()` methods that return an integer value, the `delete()` method deletes a row as pointed by our ID-based content URI object `rowUri` and returns the number of rows deleted. This will be `1` in our case as our URI points to only one row. An alternate method could be using a combination of `contentUri`, which points to the table, and `selection/selectionArgs`. In this case, the rows deleted could be more than 1 as per the `selection` clause:

```
public void delete(View v) {

      Uri contentUri = Uri.parse("content://" + AUTHORITY
                              + "/" + BASE_PATH);
      Uri rowUri = contentUri = ContentUris.withAppendedId(
                              contentUri, getFirstRowId());
      int count = getContentResolver().delete(rowUri, null,
                null);
}
```

The UI and output look like the following:

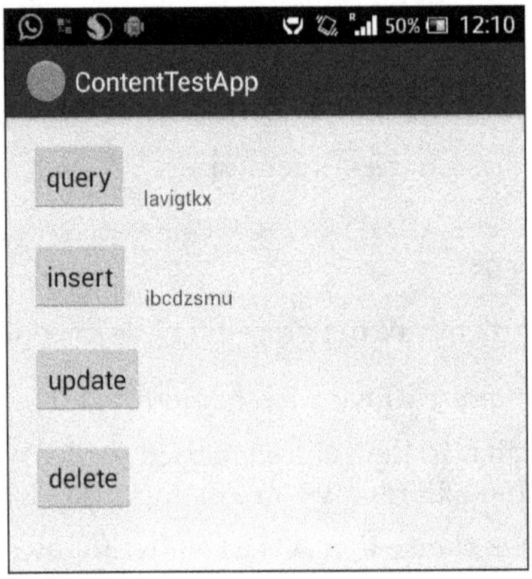

> If you want to dive in a little more into how an Android content provider actually manages various write and read calls between various tables (hint: it uses `CountDownLatch`), you can check out the video at Coursera by Dr. Douglas C. Schmidt for more information. The video can be found at `https://class.coursera.org/posa-002/lecture/49`.

Summary

In this chapter, we covered the basics of content providers. We learned how to access system-provided content providers and even our own version of a content provider. We went from creating a basic contact manager to evolving it into a fully-fledged citizen of the Android ecosystem by implementing `ContentProvider` in order to share data across other applications.

In the following chapter, we will cover `Loaders`, `CursorAdapters`, nifty hacks and tips, and some open source libraries to make our life easier while working with the SQLite database.

4
Thread Carefully

"Premature optimization is the root of all evil."

-Donald Knuth

We covered a very important concept in the previous chapter: content provider. We progressed in a step-by-step manner, covering essential questions such as how to create a content provider and how to use an existing system with a content provider in detail. We also covered how to use the content provider we created by means of creating a test application to access it.

In this chapter, we will explore how to use loaders, in particular, a loader called cursor loader. We will look at how to interact with a content provider asynchronously with the help of an example. We will discuss the important topic of security in the Android database and how we can ensure that data is secured in an Android model. Last but not least, we will also see some code snippets that will cover topics such as how to upgrade a database and how to ship a preloaded database with our application.

In this chapter, we will cover the following topics:

- Loading data with CursorLoader
- Data security
- General tips and libraries

Loading data with CursorLoader

`CursorLoader` is part of the loader family. Before we dive deep into an example explaining how to use `CursorLoader`, we will explore a bit about loaders and why it is important in the current scenario.

Loaders

Introduced in HoneyComb (API level 11), **loaders** serve the purpose of asynchronously serving data in an activity or fragment. The need to have loaders arose from many things: calls to various time-consuming methods on the main UI thread in order to fetch data that leads to a clunky UI, and even in some cases, the dreaded ANR box. This is demonstrated in the following screenshot:

For example, the `managedQuery()` method, which was deprecated in API 11, was a wrapper around the `ContentResolver'squery()` method.

In the previous chapter, while highlighting how to fetch data from a content provider inside the query method, we used `getContentResolver.query()` instead of `managedQuery()`. Using deprecated methods can lead to problems with future releases and should be avoided.

Loaders provide asynchronous loading of data for an activity of fragment on a non-UI thread. The loader or the subclasses of a loader perform their work in a separate thread and deliver their results to the main thread. The segregation of calls from the main thread and the posting of results on the main thread while working in a separate thread ensure that we have a responsive application.

> Post the loader era, we were faced with problems such as when an activity should be recreated due to a configuration change, for instance, rotation of a device's orientation. We had to worry about data and refetch data while creating a new instance. But with loaders, we don't have to worry about all these as loaders automatically reconnect to the last loader's cursor when being recreated after a device configuration change and refetch the data. As an added bonus, loaders monitor the data source and deliver new results when the content changes. In other words, loaders automatically get updated, and hence, there is no need to requery the cursor. Read more about keeping your Android application responsive and avoiding **application not responding** (**ANR**) messages at the Android developer website, `http://developer.android.com/training/articles/perf-anr.html`.

Loader API's summary

Let's look at the loader API that consists of various classes and interfaces. In this section, we will look at the implementation aspect of loader API's classes/interfaces:

Class/interface	Description
`LoaderManager`	This is an abstract class associated with an activity or fragment to manage a loader. Although there can be one or more loader instances, only one instance of `LoaderManager` per activity or fragment is permitted. It is responsible for dealing with the activity or fragment's life cycle and particularly helpful when running long-running tasks.
`LoaderManager.LoaderCallbacks`	This is a callback interface we must implement to interact with `LoaderManager`.
`Loader`	This is the base class for a loader. It's an abstract class that performs asynchronous loading of data. We can implement our own subclass instead of using subclasses such as `CursorLoader`.
`AsyncTaskLoader`	This is an abstract loader that provides `AsyncTask` to perform the work in the background, that is, on a separate thread; however, the result is delivered on the main thread. According to the documentation, it is advised to subclass `AsyncTaskLoader` instead of directly subclassing the `Loader` class.
`CursorLoader`	This is a subclass of `AsyncTaskLoader` that queries `ContentResolver` on the background thread in a non-blocking manner and returns a cursor.

Using CursorLoader

Loaders provide us with a lot of handy features; one of them is that once our activity or fragment implements a loader, it need not worry about refreshing the data. A loader monitors the data source for us, reflects any changes, and even performs new loads; all of this is done asynchronously. Hence, we do not need to take care of implementing and managing threads, offloading queries on the background thread, and retrieving results once the query is completed.

A loader can be in any one of the following three distinct states:

- **Started state**: Once started, loaders remain in this state until stopped or reset. It executes loads, monitors any change, and reflects the same to the listeners.
- **Stopped state**: Here, loaders continue to monitor changes but do not pass the result to the clients.
- **Reset state**: In this state, loaders release any resources they have held and do not perform the process of executing, loading, or monitoring data.

We will now relook at our personal contact manager application and make the corresponding changes to implement `CursorLoader` in our application. `CursorLoader`, as the name suggests, is a loader that queries `ContentResolver` and returns a cursor. This is a subclass of `AsyncTaskLoader` and performs the cursor query on the background thread so that it does not block the application's UI. In the diagram, you can see the various methods of a loader callback and how they communicate with `CursorLoader` and `CursorAdapter`.

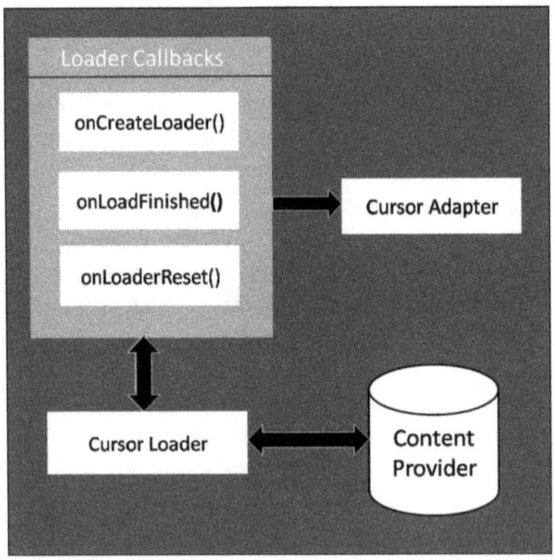

For implementing a cursor loader, we need to perform the following steps:

1. To begin with, we need to implement the `LoaderManager.LoaderCallbacks<Cursor>` interface:

   ```
   public class ContactsMainActivity extends Activity implements
   OnClickListener, LoaderManager.LoaderCallbacks<Cursor> {…}
   ```

   Then, implement the methods that reflect the distinct states of a loader: `onCreateLoader()`, `onLoadFinished()`, and `onLoaderReset()`.

2. To initiate a query, we will make a call to the `LoaderManager.initLoader()` method; this initializes the background framework:

   ```
   getLoaderManager().initLoader(CUR_LOADER, null, this);
   ```

   The `CUR_LOADER` value is passed on to the `onCreateLoader()` method, which acts as an ID for the loader. A call to `initloader()` invokes `onCreateLoader()`, passing the ID we used to call `initloader()`:

   ```
   @Override
   public Loader<Cursor> onCreateLoader(int loaderID,
   Bundle bundle)
   {
     switch (loaderID) {
     case CUR_LOADER:
       return new CursorLoader(this, PersonalContactContract.CONTENT_
   URI,
         PersonalContactContract.PROJECTION_ALL, null, null, null );
       default: return null;
     }
   }
   ```

3. We use a switch case to take the loader based on its ID and return `null` for an invalid ID. We create a URI object `contentUri` and pass it as a parameter to the `CursorLoader` constructor. A point to note is that we can implement a cursor loader using either this constructor or an empty unspecified cursor loader, `CursorLoader(Context context)`. Also, we can set values via methods such as `setUri(Uri)`, `setSelection(String)`, `setSelectionArgs(String[])`, `setSortOrder(String)`, and `setProjection(String[])`:

   ```
   public CursorLoader (Context context, Uri uri, String[] projection,
   String selection, String[] selectionArgs, String sortOrder)
   ```

   The following are the parameters of the previous code:

   - `context`: This is the parent activity context.
   - `uri`: We employ `contentURI`, using the `content://` scheme, to retrieve the content. It can be based on an ID or directory.
   - `projection`: This is a list of columns to be returned as we are prepared with the column names. Passing `null` will return all the columns.
   - `selection`: This is formatted as a SQL `WHERE` clause, excluding the `WHERE` itself, acting as a filter declaring which rows to return.

- `selectionArgs`: We may include question marks in the selection, which will be replaced by the values bound as a string from `selectionArgs`, and they will appear in the order of their selection.
- `sortOrder`: This tells us how to order rows, formatted as a SQL `ORDER BY` clause. A null value will use the default sort order.

4. `onCreateLoader` starts the query in the background, and when the query is finished, the cursor loader object is passed to the background's framework, which calls `onLoadFinished()`, where we provide our adapter instance with the cursor object data:

```
@Override
public void onLoadFinished(Loader<Cursor> loader, Cursor data)
{
  this.mAdapter.changeCursor(data);
}
```

5. The adapter is a subclass of `CursorAdapter`. Instead of the traditional `getView()` method, which we get by extending `BaseAdapter`, we have the `bindView()` and `newView()` methods. We inflate our listview row layout in the view object in `newView`, and in bind view, we perform an action similar to the `getView()` method. We define our layout elements and associate theme with the relevant data:

```
public class CustomCursorAdapter extends CursorAdapter
{
   ...
  public void bindView(View view, Context arg1, Cursor cursor)
  {
    finalImageView contact_photo = (ImageView) view
      .findViewById(R.id.contact_photo);
  ...
  ...
  contact_email.setText(cursor.getString(cursor
       .getColumnIndexOrThrow(DatabaseConstants.TABLE_ROW_
EMAIL)));
  setImage(cursor.getBlob(cursor
       .getColumnIndex(DatabaseConstants.TABLE_ROW_PHOTOID)),
      contact_photo);
   }

   @Override
  public View newView(Context arg0, Cursor arg1, ViewGroup arg2)
  {
    final View view = LayoutInflater.from(context).inflate(
```

```
        R.layout.contact_list_row, null, false);
      return view;
    }
  ...
}
```

6. This method is invoked when the cursor loader is being reset. We clear out any reference to the cursor by passing `null` to the `changeCursor()` method. Whenever the data associated with a cursor changes, the cursor loader calls this method before it reruns the query to clear any past references, thereby preventing memory leaks. Once `onLoaderReset()` is set, the cursor loader will rerun its query:

```
@Override
public void onLoaderReset(Loader<Cursor> loader)
{
  this.mAdapter.changeCursor(null);

    }
```

7. Now we move on to our content provider where we have to make small changes to ensure that any changes we make to the database are reflected in our application's list view:

```
cr.setNotificationUri(getContext().getContentResolver(),uri);
```

8. We need to register `observer` in `ContentResolver` through the cursor in the query method of `ContentProvider`. We do this to watch the content URI for any changes, which can be the URI of a specific data row or table in our case:

```
getContext().getContentResolver().notifyChange(ur,null);
```

9. In the `insert()` method, we use the `notifyChange()` method to inform registered observers that a row was updated. By default, the `CursorAdapter` objects will get this notification. So, now when we add a new row of data by inserting a new contact in our application, the `insert()` method of `contentProvider` is invoked via a call:

```
resolver.insert(PersonalContactContract.CONTENT_URI,
prepareData(contact));
```

10. A similar action needs to be performed for the `delete()` and `update()` methods, both of which have been left as an exercise for the reader as most of the boilerplate code is present. Implementing a loader is simple and saves us from a lot of headache when it comes to threading, and a jarring UI is highly recommended to perform this task.

> `loadInBackground()` is another important method; this returns a cursor instance for a load operation and is called on the worker thread. Ideally, `loadInBackground()` should not directly return the result of the load operation, but we can achieve this by overriding the `deliverResult(D)` method. To cancel, we need to check the value of `isLoadInBackgroundCanceled()` as we do in the case of `AsyncTask`, where we check `isCancelled()` periodically.

Data security

Security is the latest buzzword in town. The Android ecosystem ensures that our database is exposed to prying eyes; however, a rooted device can leave our database exposed, as we saw in *Chapter 2, Connecting the Dots*. With the help of a rooted device, an emulator and the `adb pull` command in our case, we pulled our database for inspection with the SQLite manager tool. Another important aspect is content providers; we need to be careful while setting permissions. We should make the process of applying appropriate permissions compulsory in order to inform users about the control that an app establishes over data, using the `contract` class.

ContentProvider and permissions

In *Chapter 3, Sharing is Caring*, we briefly covered the topic of permissions in the *Adding a provider to a manifest* section. Let's elaborate a little more on this:

1. As mentioned earlier, while adding the content provider to the manifest, we will also add our custom permissions. This will ensure two things, namely, stop an unauthorized action in an application and inform the users about permissions:

```
<provider
android:name="com.personalcontactmanager.provider.
PersonalContactProvider"
android:authorities="com.personalcontactmanager.provider"
android:readPermission="com.personalcontactmanager.provider.read"
android:exported="true"
android:grantUriPermissions="true"
>
```

2. Additionally, we will add the `permissions` tag to the manifest to indicate the set of permissions that other applications will require:

```
<permission
android:name="com.personalcontactmanager.provider.read"
android:icon="@drawable/ic_launcher"
```

```
android:label="Contact Manager"
android:protectionLevel="normal" >
</permission>
```

3. Now, in the application in which we want to access the content provider we use the `permission` tag, in our case, `Ch4-TestApp` in code bundle:

```
<uses-permission android:name="com.personalcontactmanager.
provider.read" />
```

   When users install this application, they will get our custom permission message along with other permissions required by the application. For this step, instead of directly running the application from Eclipse, export an apk and install it::

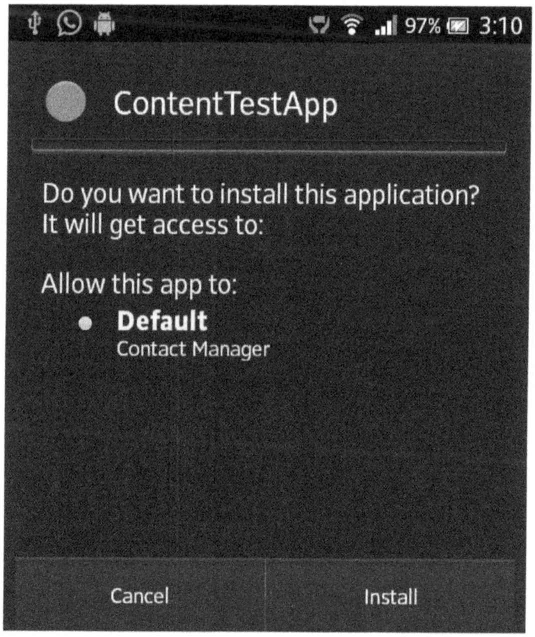

If you have not defined the permission in the application and if the application tries to access the content provider, it will get the `SecurityException: Permission Denial` message.

If the content provider we created is not meant to be shared, we will need to change the `android:exported="true"` property to `false`. This will make our content provider secure, and if someone tries to run a malicious query on it, they will encounter a security exception.

If we want to share data only between our applications, Android provides a solution; we can use `android:protectionLevel` and set the permission to `signature` instead of `normal`. For this, both the apps, the one that implements the content provider and the one that wants to access it, have to be signed by the same key while they are exported. This is because a bonus signature permission does not require user confirmation. This does not confuse the user as it is done internally and also does not obstruct the user experience.

Encrypting critical data

We have already discussed what kind of access rights other applications have on our database and how to efficiently share our content providers, and we also briefly discussed why we should not believe that the system is foolproof. In the most foolproof method, sensitive data will not be kept on the device but on the server instead, and it will use tokens to give access. If you have to store the data on the device's database, use encryption. Use a user-defined key to encrypt and decrypt sensitive data.

We will explore a way to use an encrypted database, which will not be readable if someone is able to extract it via means of a root or via exploiting backups. If someone tries to read it using SQLite Manager or some other tool, they will receive a friendly message, such as the one shown in the following screenshot; this is the database file that we will create in a moment with a library known as SQLCipher.

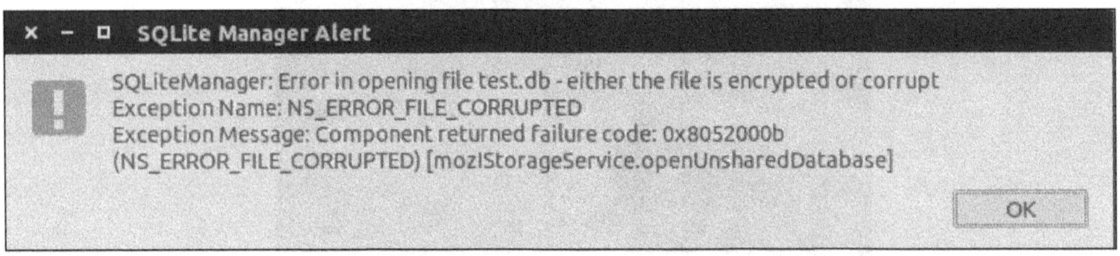

SQLCipher is an open source extension to SQLite that provides a transparent 256-bit AES encryption of database files, as mentioned on their website. It is very easy to deploy SQLCipher. Now we'll look at the steps to build a sample application:

1. First, we will download the necessary files from `http://sqlcipher.net/open-source`. Here, they have listed a community edition of the Android-based SQLCipher; download it.
2. Now we will create a new Android project in our eclipse environment.

3. Inside the downloaded folder, we will find the `libs` folder; inside it, are a set of jars that we will need to work with SQLCipher. We will also notice that folders are named as `armeabi`, `armeabi-v7a`, and `x86`, and all of these contain the `.so` files. If you are familiar with Android NDK, this will not seem new. The `.so` file is a shared object file, which is a component of dynamic libraries. For different architectures, we require different `.so` files, hence the three folders. If you are running an x86 emulator, you will need the `x86` folder in your `libs` folder. For simplicity, we will copy all the folders to the `libs` folder. Copy the `asset` folder's content into our project's `asset` folder and navigate to the project's properties. It will look something like the following screenshot. You can also see these JAR files in the project's class path. The initial setup for this project is now complete.

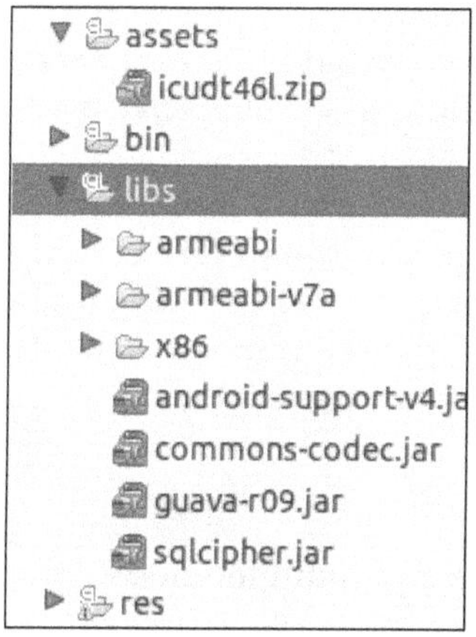

After completing the necessary setup part, let's move to writing code to make a small test application:

```
public class MainActivity extends Activity
{
  TextView showResult;

   @Override
   protected void onCreate(Bundle savedInstanceState)
   {
super.onCreate(savedInstanceState);
  setContentView(R.layout.activity_main);
  showResult = (TextView) findViewById(R.id.showResult);
  InitializeSQLCipher();
   }

   private void InitializeSQLCipher()
```

```
    {
SQLiteDatabase.loadLibs(this);
  File databaseFile = getDatabasePath("test.db");
  databaseFile.mkdirs();
  databaseFile.delete();
  SQLiteDatabase database = SQLiteDatabase
      .openOrCreateDatabase(databaseFile, "test123", null);
  database.execSQL("create table t1(a, b)");
  database.execSQL("insert into t1(a, b) values(?, ?)",
        new Object[] {"I am ", "Encrypted" });
    }

    public void runQuery(View v)
    {
  File databaseFile = getDatabasePath("test.db");
  SQLiteDatabase database = SQLiteDatabase.openOrCreateDatabase(
      databaseFile, "test123", null);
  String selection = "select * from t1";
  Cursor c = database.rawQuery(selection, null);
  c.moveToFirst();
  showResult.setText(c.getString(c.getColumnIndex("a")) +
c.getString(c.getColumnIndex("b")));
     }
}
```

The preceding code has two main methods: `InitializeSQLCipher()` and `runQuery()`. Inside `InitializeSQLCipher()`, we load our `.so` library files by invoking the `loadLibs()` method.

4. Now we find the absolute path to the database and create a missing parent folder if any. With `openOrCreateDatabase()`, we will make a call to open an existing database or create one if the database is nonexistent. We will execute standard database calls to create a table with columns `a` and `b` and insert values in a row.

   Now we will perform a simple query to fetch the values back to the `runQuery()` method. You will notice that apart from loading the library, all the core methods we used are pretty much standard, so where is the major change? Go to the `Ch4-PersonalContactManager` example in the code bundle and notice the packages we have used:

   ```
   import android.database.Cursor;
   import android.database.sqlite.SQLiteDatabase;
   ```

   We have SQLCipher packages:

```
import net.sqlcipher.Cursor;
import net.sqlcipher.database.SQLiteDatabase;
```

The implementation is simple, familiar, and easy to implement. If you pull the database out and try to read it, you will find the error message, as we displayed earlier in a screenshot. The user will find no change, and even our app's logic remains the same. In the screenshot, you can see the application screen we just built which encrypts the database:

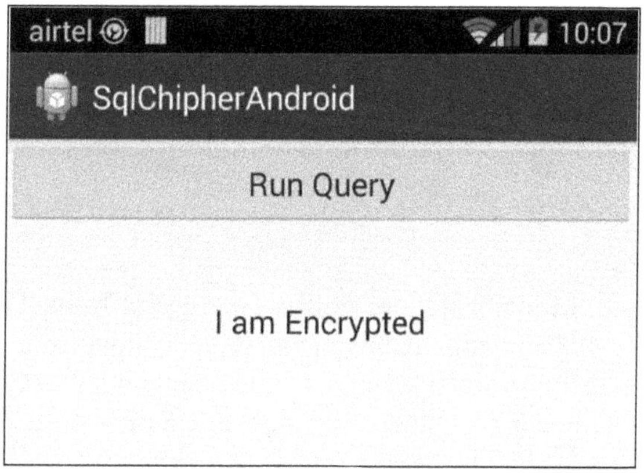

> **OAuth** is an open standard for authorization. It provides client applications with a *secure delegated access* to server resources on behalf of a resource owner. It specifies a process for resource owners to authorize third-party access to their server resources without sharing their credentials, as explained in Wikipedia; read more about OAuth at `http://oauth.net/2/`.

General tips and libraries

We will cover some general and not so general workarounds and practices, which can be put to good use depending on the situation. For instance, in some cases, we need to have a prepopulated database of values that we will make use of in our Android application or upgrading a database, which seems trivial but can break our application.

Upgrading a database

In *Chapter 2, Connecting the Dots,* we used `onUpgrade()` to show how a database is updated. If we go back to the example, you will notice that it executes a `Drop Table` command. What will happen here is that the original table will be dropped and a new table will be created by the call, `onCreate()`. This will lead to a loss of the existing data and hence is not suitable if we need to alter our database. The `onUpgrade()` function can be defined as follows:

```
public void onUpgrade(SQLiteDatabase db, int oldVersion,int
newVersion)
{
  String DROP_TABLE = "DROP TABLE IF EXISTS " + TABLE_NAME;
  db.execSQL(DROP_TABLE);
  onCreate(db);
}
```

One more challenge is to identify the version we are using here. The user might be running older versions of the application, so we have to keep in mind the different versions that an application has and whether those versions would bring about any changes in the database. For a new user, we need not worry because if the database does not exist, `onCreate()` will be called.

To make sure we have a proper upgrade, we will use the `DB_VERSION` constant in our `CustomSQLiteOpenHelper` class to tell our `onUpgrade()` method about the action to be taken:

```
private static final int DB_VERSION = 1;
```

We will change the `DB_VERSION` constant to `3` to reflect the upgrade:

```
private static final int DB_VERSION = 3;
```

The constructor will take care of the rest:

```
public CustomSQLiteOpenHelper(Context context)
{
  super(context, DB_NAME, null, DB_VERSION);
}
```

When the super class constructor is run, it compares the `DB_VERSION` constant of the stored SQLite `.db` file against the `DB_VERSION` we passed as a parameter and calls the `onUpgrade()` method if needed:

```
public void onUpgrade(SQLiteDatabase db, int oldVersion,int
newVersion)
```

```
{
switch(oldVersion) {
   case 1: db.execSQL(DATABASE_CREATE_MAIN_TABLE);
   case 2: db.execSQL(DATABASE_CREATE_MAIN_TABLE);
   case 3: db.execSQL(DATABASE_CREATE_DEL_TABLE);
   }
}
```

Inside our `onUpgrade()` method, we have a switch case to make changes. Notice that we do not use the `break` statement because the user can be on an older version and may not have updated the application, as explained earlier. For instance, let's consider that a user is on a particular version of an application that is running `DB_VERSION =1` and he or she skips the next update that contained `DB_VERSION =2`, and eventually, a new version of the application with `DB_VERSION =3` is released. Now, we have a case where the user is still using an older version of the application and has not installed the new updates we have released. So, in this case, when the user installs the application, the `onUpgrade()` method will first execute `case 1` and then go to `case 2` to install updates that the user missed; finally, the user will install the updates of the third version, ensuring that all the database changes are reflected. Notice that there is no `break` statement. This is because we want to run all the cases where the `switch` statement obtains the value `1` and the last two statements where the switch case obtains the value `2`.

Alternatively, we can also use the `if` statement. This will also behave as we intended as our test `DB_VERSION` constant was `1`, which will satisfy both the conditions and reflect the changes:

```
if (oldVersion<2) {db.execSQL(DATABASE_CREATE_MORE_TABLE); }
if (oldVersion<3) {db.execSQL(DATABASE_CREATE_DEL_TABLE); }
```

Database minus SQL statements

In most parts of the book, we looked around for nooks and corners of Android and SQLite. For some, writing SQL statements would be just another day in the office, while for some, it will come across as a roller-coaster ride. This section will cover a library that enables us to save and retrieve SQLite database records without writing a single SQL statement. **ActiveAndroid** is an active record-style SQLite persistence for Android. According to the documentation, each database record is wrapped neatly into a class with methods such as `save()` and `delete()`. We will be using the example in the ActiveAndroid documentation and build a working sample based on it. Let's look at the steps required to get it up and running.

Have a look at the official site, `http://www.activeandroid.com/`, for an overview and download the files from `http://goo.gl/oW2kod`.

Once you download the file, run `ant` on the root folder to build the JAR file. Once you run `ant`, you will find your JAR file in the `dist` folder. In Eclipse, make a new project, add the JAR file to the `libs` folder of the project, and then add the JAR file to the **Java Build Path** in the project properties.

ActiveAndroid looks out for some global settings configured by performing the following steps:

1. We will start by creating a class, extending the application class:

```
public class MyApplication extends com.activeandroid.app.
Application
{
   @Override
public void onCreate()
{
     super.onCreate();
     ActiveAndroid.initialize(this);
    }

   @Override
public void onTerminate()
{
     super.onTerminate();
     ActiveAndroid.dispose();
   }

}
```

2. Now we will add this application class to our manifest file and add metadata corresponding to our application:

```
<application
  android:name="com.active.android.MyApplication">
  <meta-data
     android:name="AA_DB_NAME"
     android:value="test.db" />
  <meta-data
     android:name="AA_DB_VERSION"
     android:value="1" />
.........
</application>
```

3. With this basic setup complete, we will now proceed on to creating our data model. The ActiveAndroid library supports annotation and we will use it in the following model classes:

```
// Category class

@Table(name = "Categories")
public class Category extends Model
{
@Column(name = "Name")
public String name;
}


// Item class

@Table(name = "Items")
public class Item extends Model
{
   // If name is omitted, then the field name is used.
@Column(name = "Name")
public String name;

@Column(name = "Category")
public Category category;

public Item()
{
     super();
   }

   public Item(String name, Category category)
   {
     super();
     this.name = name;
     this.category = category;
   }
   }
```

> If you want to explore annotations and use them in your project and reduce boilerplate code, you can check out the following libraries for Android: Android Annotations, Square's Dagger, and ButterKnife.

4. To add a new category or item, we need to make a call to `save()`. In the code segment, we can see that an item object is created and associated with a particular category, and in the end, `save()` is called:

   ```
   public void insert(View v)
   {
     Item testItem = new Item();
     testItem.category = testCategory;
     testItem.name = editTextItem.getText().toString();
     testItem.save();
   }
   ```

   To delete an item, we can call `item.delete()`. Similarly, to fetch values, we have relevant methods as well. The following is a call to fetch all of the data for a particular category:

   ```
   List<Item>getall = new Select().from(Item.class)
         .where("Category = ?", testCategory.getId())
         .orderBy("Name ASC").execute();
   ```

There is lot more to be explored in ActiveAndroid. They have schema migration and type serialization; in addition to this, you can ship a prepopulated database by placing the database in the `asset` folder, and you can use content providers as well. In short, it is a well-built library for people looking for indirect ways to communicate with the database and perform database operations. It helps in accessing the database in the familiar form of Java methods instead of preparing SQL statements to perform the same action. The complete sample code is bundled in the `chapter 4` code bundle.

Shipping with a prepopulated database

We will build a database and put it inside our `asset` folder, which is a read-only directory. At runtime, we will check whether a database exists. If not, we will copy our database from the `asset` folder to `/data/data/yourpackage/databases`. In *Chapter 2, Connecting the Dots*, we used a tool called SQLite Manager; have a look at the third screenshot of the chapter. We are going to use the same tool to build our database now. If you pull your database as explained in that section or look at that screenshot, you will notice a few more tables along with your database table:

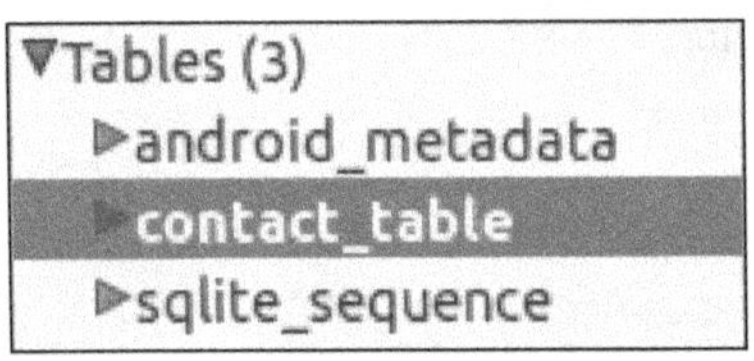

The steps to be followed to create a prepopulated database are as follows:

1. To make a prepopulated database, we need to create a table named `android_metadata` apart from the table we require. Using the SQLite Manager tool, we will create a new database named `contact`, then we will create the `android_metdata` table:

   ```
   CREATE TABLE "android_metadata"("locale" TEXT DEFAULT 'en_US')
   ```

2. We will insert a row in the table:

   ```
   INSERT INTO "android_metadata" VALUES ('en_US')
   ```

3. Now we will create the tables we require, in our case, `contact_table` using the SQL query we used in *Chapter 2, Connecting the Dots*. In the `DatabaseManager` class, we will just replace the constants with the actual values:

   ```
   CREATE TABLE "contact_table" ("_id" integer primary key
   autoincrement not null,"contact_name" text not null,"contact_
   number" text not null,"contact_email" text not null,"photo_id"
   BLOB )
   ```

   It is necessary to rename the primary ID field of our tables to `_id` if it is not already defined. This helps Android in identifying where to bind the ID field of our tables.

4. Let us fill a few rows of data. We can do this by running the `Insert` query or manually typing in the values using the tool. Now, copy the database file into the `asset` folder.
5. Now, in our original personal contact manager, we will modify our `DatabaseManager` class. The good part is that this is the only class we need to modify and the rest of the system will work as intended.
6. When the application runs and creates a new `DatabaseManager` class by passing the context, we will make a call to `createDatabase()` in which first of all we will check whether the database already exists:

   ```
   Private Boolean checkDataBase()
   {
     SQLiteDatabase checkDB = null;
     try {
        String myPath = DB_PATH + DB_NAME;
        checkDB = SQLiteDatabase.openDatabase(myPath, null,
            SQLiteDatabase.OPEN_READONLY);
     } catch (SQLiteException e) {
        // database doesn't exist yet.
     }
   ```

```
    if (checkDB != null) {
        checkDB.close();
    }
    return checkDB != null ? true : false;
}
```

7. If it doesn't, we will create an empty database that we will replace with our database, which we copied into our `asset` folder. After copying the database from the `asset` folder, we will create a new `SQLiteDatabase` object:

```
private void copyDataBase() throws IOException
{
  InputStream myInput = myContext.getAssets().open(DB_NAME);
  String outFileName = DB_PATH + DB_NAME;
  OutputStream myOutput = new FileOutputStream(outFileName);
  byte[] buffer = new byte[1024];
  int length;
  while ((length = myInput.read(buffer)) > 0) {
     myOutput.write(buffer, 0, length);
  }

  myOutput.flush();
  myOutput.close();
  myInput.close();
}
```

Another point to note is that the `onCreate()` method of our `CustomSQLiteOpenHelper` class will be empty as we are not creating a database and tables, but we are copying one. The sample code is bundled in the `chapter 4` code bundle. If this process looks tedious, don't worry; the Android developers' community has a solution for you. SQLiteAssetHelper is an Android library that will help you in managing database creation and version management, using an application's raw asset files.

To implement this, we have to follow a few simple steps:

1. Copy the JAR file into our project's `libs` folder.
2. Add a library to Java Build Path.
3. Copy our zipped database file into the `asset` folder of `projectassets/databases/your_database.db.zip`.
4. The ZIP file should contain only one `db` file.
5. Instead of extending the framework's `SQLiteOpenHelper` class, we will extend the `SQLiteAssetHelper` class.

6. They also provide you with assistance to upgrade the database file, which needs to be placed in assets/databases/<database_name>_upgrade_<from_version>-<to_version>.sql.
7. The library, documentation, and its corresponding sample can be found at http://goo.gl/8XSSmR.

Summary

We covered a myriad of advanced topics in this chapter, ranging from loaders to the security of data. We implemented our cursor loader to understand how a loader works magic for our applications, and we delved into securing our database and understanding the concept of permissions while exposing our content provider to other applications. We also covered some tips such as shipping with a prepopulated database, upgrading a database without breaking the system, and using database queries without using SQL commands. This is in no way the only set of things we can achieve with database and Android. This chapter only serves as a nudge towards the vast programming possibilities out there.

Index

D

E

F

G

T

U

V

Thank you for buying

Android SQLite Essentials

About Packt Publishing

Packt, pronounced 'packed', published its first book "*Mastering phpMyAdmin for Effective MySQL Management*" in April 2004 and subsequently continued to specialize in publishing highly focused books on specific technologies and solutions.

Our books and publications share the experiences of your fellow IT professionals in adapting and customizing today's systems, applications, and frameworks. Our solution based books give you the knowledge and power to customize the software and technologies you're using to get the job done. Packt books are more specific and less general than the IT books you have seen in the past. Our unique business model allows us to bring you more focused information, giving you more of what you need to know, and less of what you don't.

Packt is a modern, yet unique publishing company, which focuses on producing quality, cutting-edge books for communities of developers, administrators, and newbies alike. For more information, please visit our website: `www.packtpub.com`.

About Packt Open Source

In 2010, Packt launched two new brands, Packt Open Source and Packt Enterprise, in order to continue its focus on specialization. This book is part of the Packt Open Source brand, home to books published on software built around Open Source licenses, and offering information to anybody from advanced developers to budding web designers. The Open Source brand also runs Packt's Open Source Royalty Scheme, by which Packt gives a royalty to each Open Source project about whose software a book is sold.

Writing for Packt

We welcome all inquiries from people who are interested in authoring. Book proposals should be sent to `author@packtpub.com`. If your book idea is still at an early stage and you would like to discuss it first before writing a formal book proposal, contact us; one of our commissioning editors will get in touch with you.

We're not just looking for published authors; if you have strong technical skills but no writing experience, our experienced editors can help you develop a writing career, or simply get some additional reward for your expertise.

Instant Spring for Android Starter

ISBN: 978-1-78216-190-5 Paperback: 72 pages

Leverage Spring for Android to create RESTful and OAuth Android apps

1. Learn something new in an Instant! A short, fast, focused guide delivering immediate results.
2. Learn what Spring for Android adds to the Android developer toolkit.
3. Learn how to debug your Android communication layer observing HTTP requests and responses.

Android Application Security Essentials

ISBN: 978-1-84951-560-3 Paperback: 218 pages

Write secure Android applications using the most up-to-date techniques and concepts

1. Understand Android security from kernel to the application layer.
2. Protect components using permissions.
3. Safeguard user and corporate data from prying eyes.
4. Understand the security implications of mobile payments, NFC, and more.

Please check **www.PacktPub.com** for information on our titles

CPSIA information can be obtained
at www.ICGtesting.com
Printed in the USA
FSHW021443060820
72682FS